1 MONTH OF
FREE
READING

at

www.ForgottenBooks.com

By purchasing this book you are eligible for one month membership to ForgottenBooks.com, giving you unlimited access to our entire collection of over 1,000,000 titles via our web site and mobile apps.

To claim your free month visit:
www.forgottenbooks.com/free864596

ISBN 978-0-265-54871-4
PIBN 10864596

GUIDE

TO THE

CRYSTAL PALACE AND PARK.

CONVEYANCE BY RAIL AND ROAD FROM LONDON.

THE CRYSTAL PALACE BY RAILWAY.

TRAINS conveying persons direct to the Palace leave the Bridge Terminus of the Brighton Railway at a quarter before nine in the morning on Mondays, and a quarter before ten on Tuesdays, Wednesdays, and Thursdays, and continue running every quarter of an hour, or more frequently when occasion requires, throughout the day : returning from the palace every quarter of an hour, and in the evening until all the visitors desirous of travelling to Town by railway have quitted the building, which closes one hour before sunset. The Fares to the Palace and back, including admission to the Palace itself, are, on the above days, two shillings and sixpence, *first class;* two shillings, *second class;* and one shilling and sixpence, *third class.*

On Fridays and Saturdays the Crystal Palace opens at twelve o'clock in the morning, and trains will start from London at a quarter before that hour, and continue running every quarter of an hour throughout the day, returning every quarter of an hour until all the visitors shall have quitted the Palace.

Holders of season tickets will be conveyed from London by train to the Palace on every day of the week by payment of the ordinary fare of the Brighton Railway.

Omnibuses from all parts of London will convey passengers direct to the terminus of the Brighton Railway.

Visitors residing at or desirous of reaching the Palace from the New Cross or Forest Hill stations, on the Brighton line, will be conveyed to the Palace by the ordinary Epsom and Croydon trains, which leave London at quick intervals, and call at both these stations. These trains will, however, convey them only to the Anerley or Sydenham stations, from which places conveyances to the Palace may be procured.

THE CRYSTAL PALACE BY ROAD.

Persons travelling in carriages from London to the Palace will find the various roads marked on the annexed map, which will enable them to choose the most expeditious routes from different parts of the metropolis to the Crystal Palace doors. Carriages from London must set down at either the north or south transepts, but not at the central transept; whilst visitors from Penge, Beckenham, and all places situated to the south-east of the Palace, will set down at the Crystal Palace Railway station.

The Crystal Palace Company have already provided accommodation for three hundred horses, in the "Paxton Stables," at the Woodman Inn, on Westow Hill, within five minutes' walk of the Palace. The charge for such accommodation is fixed at one shilling and sixpence, including a feed of corn and all other expenses, no attendant being allowed to receive a fee. Carriages and horses will find a convenient stand formed in front of the Palace, opposite the north and south transepts, where horses will be supplied with hay and water at a very trifling charge.

All communications concerning the road traffic to the Palace should be addressed to Mr. Charles Bourner, Traffic Manager, Crystal Palace, Sydenham.

VIEW OF BUILDING FROM THE NORTH.

GUIDE

TO THE

CRYSTAL PALACE

AND

PARK.

By SAMUEL PHILLIPS.

ILLUSTRATED BY P. H. DELAMOTTE.

CRYSTAL PALACE LIBRARY;
AND
BRADBURY AND EVANS, 11, BOUVERIE STREET, LONDON.
1854.

BRADBURY AND EVANS,
PRINTERS TO THE CRYSTAL PALACE COMPANY
WHITEFRIARS.

CONTENTS.

PREFACE.

THE following pages are presented to the public as a brief but connected and carefully prepared account of the exterior and interior of the Crystal Palace. It is believed that no important or interesting object in connexion with the Exhibition is without its record in this little volume; although, in so vast a collection of works of architecture, sculpture, and industrial manufacture, it is clearly impossible to compress within the limits of a General Handbook all the information which is necessary to satisfy the visitor desirous of precise and accurate knowledge of the numberless objects offered to his contemplation.

A general and comprehensive view of the Crystal Palace will unquestionably be obtained by the perusal of the present manual. The Hand-books of the respective departments will supply all the detailed information necessary to fill in the broad and rapidly drawn outlines. In them, Literature will faithfully serve as the handmaiden to Art, and complete the great auxiliary work of education which it is the first aim of the Crystal Palace to effect.

These Hand-books are published at prices varying from three-pence to eighteen-pence, according to the size of the volume. The lowest possible price has been affixed to one and all. It may be fearlessly asserted that books containing the same amount of entertainment, information, and instruction, it would be difficult to purchase at a more reasonable rate elsewhere.

The Crystal Palace—destined for permanent service—opens incomplete with respect to a part of its design. The public will not be the losers by the circumstance. With the exception of the great water displays—which are already far advanced, and will rapidly be brought to completion—the grand scheme originally projected by the Directors has been, in its chief features, thoroughly carried out by their officers. It would have been physically impossible to accomplish more than has been done. What has been achieved, within comparatively a few months, must elicit admiration and astonishment. Already the Crystal Palace stands unrivalled for the size and character of its structure, for the nature of its contents, and for the extent and advancing beauty of its pleasure-grounds. Day by day the people will have an opportunity of witnessing the growth of their Palace, and the extension of its means of good. An institution intended to last for ages, and to widen the scope, and to brighten the path, of education throughout the land, must have time to consolidate its own powers of action, and to complete its own system of instruction. Within a very few months, the promises held out from the first by the Directors will be fulfilled to the very letter; and the community may, in the meanwhile, watch the progress of the Crystal Palace towards the certain accomplishment of its unprecedented design.

INTRODUCTION.

THE annexed map of the routes to the Crystal Palace will enable the visitor to ascertain the shortest and least troublesome way of reaching the Palace from the various parts of the great metropolis and its environs. For his further information full particulars are added respecting the times of starting, and the fares of the journey by the London and Brighton Railway, which will serve as the great main line for the conveyance of visitors by rail from London to the Palace doors.

We will presume that the visitor has taken his railway ticket, which, for his convenience, includes admission within the Palace, and that his short ten minutes' journey has commenced. Before he alights, and whilst his mind is still unoccupied by the wonders that are to meet his eye, we take the opportunity to relate, as briefly as we can, the History of the Crystal Palace, from the day upon which the Royal Commissioners assembled within its transparent walls to declare their great and successful mission ended, until the 10th of June, 1854, when reconstructed, and renewed and beautified in all its proportions, it again opened its wide doors to continue and confirm the good it had already effected in the nation and beyond it.

It will be remembered that the destination of the Great Exhibition building occupied much public attention towards the close of 1851, and that a universal regret prevailed at the threatened loss of a structure which had accomplished so much for the improvement of the national taste, and which was evidently capable, under intelligent direction, of effecting so very much more. A special commission even had been appointed for the purpose of reporting on the different useful purposes to which the building could be applied, and upon the cost necessary to carry them out. Further discussion on the subject, however, was rendered unnecessary by the declaration of the Home Secretary, on the 25th of March, 1852, that Government had determined not to interfere in any way with the building, which accordingly remained, according to previous agreement, in the hands of Messrs. Fox and Henderson, the builders and contractors. Notwithstanding the announcement of the Home Secretary, a last public effort towards rescuing the Crystal Palace for its original site in Hyde Park, was made by Mr. Heywood in the House of Commons, on the 29th of April. But Government again declined the responsibility of purchasing the structure, and Mr. Heywood's motion was, by a large majority, lost.

It was at this juncture that Mr. Leech,* a private gentleman, conceived the idea of rescuing the edifice from destruction, and of rebuilding it on some appropriate spot, by the organization of a private company. On communicating this view to his partner, Mr. Farquhar, he received from him a ready and cordial approval. They then submitted their project to Mr. Francis Fuller, who entering into their views, undertook and arranged, on their joint behalf, a conditional purchase from Messrs. Fox and Henderson, of the Palace as it stood. In the belief that a building, so destined, would, if erected on a metropolitan line of railway, greatly conduce to the interests of the line, and that communication by railway was essential for the conveyance thither of great masses from London, Mr. Farquhar next suggested to Mr. Leo Schuster, a Director of the Brighton Railway, that a site for the new Palace should be selected on the Brighton line. Mr. Schuster, highly approving of the conception, obtained the hearty concurrence of Mr. Laing, the Chairman of the Brighton Board, and of his brother Directors, for aiding as far as possible in the prosecution of

* Of the firm of Johnston, Farquhar, and Leech, Solicitors.

the work. And, accordingly, these five gentlemen, and their immediate friends determined forthwith to complete the purchase of the building. On the 24th of May, 1852, the purchase-money was paid, and a few English gentlemen became the owners of the Crystal Palace of 1851. Their names follow :—

Original Purchasers of the Building.

MR. T. N. FARQUHAR,	MR. JOSEPH LEECH,
MR. FRANCIS FULLER,	MR. J. C. MORICE,
MR. ROBERT GILL,	MR. SCOTT RUSSELL,
MR. HARMAN GRISEWOOD,	MR. LEO SCHUSTER.

MR. SAMUEL LAING,

It will hardly be supposed that these gentlemen had proceeded thus far without having distinctly considered the final destination of their purchase. They decided that the building,—the first wonderful example of a new style of architecture—should rise again greatly enhanced in grandeur and beauty; that it should form a Palace for the multitude, where, at all times, protected from the inclement varieties of our climate, healthful exercise and wholesome recreation should be easily attainable. To raise the enjoyments and amusements of the English people, and especially to afford to the inhabitants of London, in wholesome country air, amidst the beauties of nature, the elevating treasures of art, and the instructive marvels of science, an accessible and inexpensive substitute for the injurious and debasing amusements of a crowded metropolis :—to blend for them instruction with pleasure, to educate them by the eye, to quicken and purify their taste by the habit of recognising the beautiful—to place them amidst the trees, flowers, and plants of all countries and of all climates, and to attract them to the study of the natural sciences, by displaying their most interesting examples—and making known all the achievements of modern industry, and the marvels of mechanical manufactures:—such were some of the original intentions of the first promoters of this National undertaking.

Having decided upon their general design, and upon the scale on which it should be executed, the directors next proceeded to select the officers to whom the carrying out of the work should be entrusted. Sir JOSEPH PAXTON, the inventive architect of the great building in Hyde Park, was requested to accept the office of Director of the Winter Garden, Park, and Conservatory, an office of which the duties became subsequently much more onerous and extensive than the title implies. Mr. OWEN JONES and Mr. DIGBY WYATT, who had distinguished themselves by their labours in the old Crystal Palace, accepted the duties of Directors of the Fine Art Department, and of the decorations of the new structure. Mr. CHARLES WILD, the engineer of the old building, filled the same office in the new one. Mr. GROVE, the secretary of the Society of Arts, the parent institution of the Exhibition of 1851, was appointed secretary. Mr. FRANCIS FULLER, a member of the Hyde Park Executive Committee, accepted the duties of managing director. Mr. SAMUEL LAING, M.P., the Chairman of the Brighton Railway Company, became Chairman also of the New Crystal Palace, and Messrs. Fox and HENDERSON undertook the re-erection of the building.

With these arrangements, a Company was formed, under the name of the Crystal Palace Company, and a prospectus issued, announcing the proposed capital of 500,000l., in one hundred thousand shares of five pounds each. The following gentlemen constituted the Board of Directors, and they have continued in office up to the present time :—

SAMUEL LAING, Esq., M.P., Chairman.

ARTHUR ANDERSON, Esq.,   CHARLES GEACH, Esq., M.P.,
E. S. P. CALVERT, Esq.,   CHARLES LUSHINGTON, Esq.,
T. N. FARQUHAR, Esq.,   J. SCOTT RUSSELL, Esq., F.R.S.,
         FRANCIS FULLER, Esq., Managing Director.

It will ever be mentioned, to the credit of the English people, that within a fortnight after the issue of the Company's prospectus, the shares were taken up to an extent that gave the Directors ample encouragement to proceed vigorously with their novel and gigantic undertaking.

In the prospectus it was proposed to transfer the building to Sydenham, in Kent, and the site chosen was an irregular parallelogram of three hundred acres,* extending from the Brighton Railway to the road which forms the boundary of the Dulwich wood at the top of the hill, the fall from which to the railway is two hundred feet. It was at once felt that the summit of this hill was the only position, in all the ground, for the great glass building—a position which, on the one side, commands a beautiful view of the fine counties of Surrey and Kent, and on the other a prospect of the great metropolis. This site was chosen, and we doubt whether a finer is to be found so close to London, and so easy of access by means of railway. To facilitate the conveyance of passengers, the Brighton Railway Company,—under special and mutually advantageous arrangements—undertook to lay down a new line of rails between London and Sydenham, to construct a branch from the Sydenham station to the Crystal Palace garden, and to build a number of engines sufficiently powerful to draw heavy trains up the steep incline to the Palace.

And now the plans were put into practical and working shape. The building was to gain in strength and artistic effect, whilst the contents of the mighty structure were to be most varied. Art was to be worthily represented by Architecture and Sculpture. Architectural restorations were to be made, and Architectural specimens from the most remarkable edifices throughout the world, to be collected, in order to present a grand architectural sequence from the earliest dawn of the art down to the latest times. Casts of the most celebrated works of Sculpture were to be procured : so that within the glass walls might be seen a vast historical gallery of this branch of art, from the time of the ancient Egyptians to our own era. Nature also was to put forth her beauty throughout the Palace and Grounds. A magnificent collection of plants of every land was to adorn the glass structure within, whilst in the gardens the fountains of Versailles

* A portion of this land, not required for the purposes of the Palace, has been disposed of.

were to be outrivalled, and Englishmen at length enabled to witness
the water displays, which for years had proved a source of pleasure
and recreation to foreigners in their own countries. Nor was this all.
All those sciences, an acquaintance with which is attainable through
the medium of the eye, were allotted their specific place, and Geology,
Ethnology, and Zoology were taken as best susceptible of illustration ; Professor Edward Forbes, Dr. Latham, Professor Ansted,
Mr. Waterhouse, Mr. Gould, and other gentlemen well known in
the scientific world, undertaking to secure the material basis
upon which the intellectual service was to be grounded.   To prevent
the monotony that attaches to a mere museum arrangement, in
which glass cases are ordinarily the most prominent features, the
whole of the collected objects, whether of science, art or nature,
were to be arranged in picturesque groupings, and harmony was to
reign throughout.   To give weight to their proceedings, and to
secure lasting advantage to the public, a charter was granted by
Lord Derby's government on the 28th of January, 1853, binding
the Directors and their successors to preserve the high moral and
social tone which, from the outset, they had assumed for their
National Institution.

The building paid for, the officers retained, the plans put on paper
—the work of removal now commenced, and Messrs. Fox and
Henderson received instructions to convey the palace to its destined
home at Sydenham.   The first column of the new structure was
raised by Mr. Laing, M.P., the chairman of the Company, on the
5th August, 1852 ; the works were at once proceeded with, and
the most active and strenuous efforts thenceforth made towards the
completion of the undertaking.   Shortly after the erection of the
first column, Messrs. Owen Jones and Digby Wyatt were charged
with a mission to the continent, in order to procure examples of
the principal works of art in Europe.   They were fortified by Lord
Malmesbury, then Secretary of State, with letters to the several
ambassadors on their route, expressing the sympathy of the
Government in the object of their travels, and backed by the
liberal purse of the Company, who required, for themselves, only

that the collection should prove worthy of the nation for which they were caterers.

The travellers first of all visited Paris, and received the most cordial co-operation of the Government, and of the authorities at the Museum of the Louvre, and the École des Beaux Arts. The permission to obtain casts of any objects, which could with safety be taken, was at once accorded them. From Paris they proceeded to Italy, and thence to Germany, in both which countries they experienced, generally, a ready and generous compliance with their wishes. At Munich they received especial attention, and were most kindly assisted by the British Ambassador, and the architect Baron von Klenze, through whose instrumentality and influence King Louis permitted casts of the most choice objects in the Glyptothek for the first time to be taken.

The chief exceptions to the general courtesy were at Rome, Padua, and Vienna. At the first-named city every arrangement had been made for procuring casts of the great Obelisk of the Lateran, the celebrated antique equestrian statue of Marcus Aurelius on the Capitol, the beautiful monuments by Andrea Sansovino in the church of S. M. del Popolo, the interesting bas-reliefs from the arch of Titus, and other works, when an order from the Papal Government forbade the copies to be taken : and, accordingly, for the present, our collection, as regards these valuable subjects, is incomplete.

At Padua contracts had been made for procuring that master-piece of Renaissance art, the candelabrum of Riccio, the entire series of bronzes by Donatello, and several other important works in the church of St. Anthony ; but, in spite of numerous appeals, aided by the influence of Cardinal Wiseman, the capitular authorities refused their consent.

At Vienna agreements had been entered into for procuring a most important series of monuments from the Church of St. Stephen, in that city ; including the celebrated stone pulpit, and the monument of Frederic III. A contract had also been made for obtaining a cast of the grand bronze statue of Victory, at

Brescia ; but although the influence of Lord Malmesbury and Lord Westmoreland (our ambassador at Vienna) was most actively exerted, permission was absolutely refused by the Austrian authorities in Lombardy, as well as in Vienna itself. Thus much it is necessary to state in order to justify the directors of the Crystal Palace in the eyes of the world for omissions in their collection which hitherto they have not had power to make good. They are not without hope, however, that the mere announcement of these deficiencies will be sufficient to induce the several governments to take a kindly view of the requests that have been made to them, and to participate in the satisfaction that follows every endeavour to advance human enjoyment.

In England, wherever application has been made, permission —with one exception—has been immediately granted by the authorities, whether ecclesiastical or civil, to take casts of any monuments required. The one interesting exception deserves a special record. The churchwardens of Beverley Minster, Yorkshire, enjoy the privilege of being able to refuse a cast of the celebrated Percy shrine, the most complete example of purely English art in our country ; and in spite of the protestations of the Archbishop of York, the Duke of Northumberland, Archdeacon Wilberforce, Sir Charles Barry and others, half the churchwardens in question insist, to this hour, upon their right to have their enjoyment without molestation. The visitors to the Crystal Palace cannot therefore, as yet, see the Percy shrine.

Whilst Messrs. Jones and Wyatt were busy abroad, the authorities were no less occupied at home. Sir Joseph Paxton commenced operations by securing for the Company the extensive and celebrated collection of palms and other plants, brought together with the labour of a century, by Messrs. Loddiges, of Hackney. The valuable assistance of Mr. Fergusson and Mr. Layard, M.P., was obtained for the erection of a Court to illustrate the architecture of the long-buried buildings of Assyria ; and a large space in the Gardens was devoted to illustrating the geology of the antediluvian period, and exhibiting specimens of the gigantic animals living before the flood.

As soon as the glass structure was sufficiently advanced, the valuable productions of art which Messrs. Jones and Wyatt had acquired abroad rapidly arrived, and being received into the building, the erection of the Fine Art Courts commenced. To carry out these works, artizans of almost every continental nation, together with workmen of our own country have been employed, and it is worthy of note, that, although but a few years before, many of the nations to which these men belonged, were engaged in deadly warfare against each other, and some of them opposed to our own country, yet, in the Crystal Palace, these workmen have laboured for months, side by side, with the utmost good feeling, and without the least display of national jealousy—a fact alike honourable to the men, and gratifying to all, inasmuch as it shows how completely the ill-will that formerly separated nation from nation and man from man, is dying out, and how easily those, who have been at one time enemies on the field of battle, may become fast friends in the Palace of Peace.

To the whole of these workmen, foreigners and English, engaged in the Crystal Palace, the Directors are anxious to express their obligations and sincere acknowledgments. They recognise the value of their labours, and are fully aware that, if to the minds of a Few the public are indebted for the conception of the grand Idea now happily realized, to the Many we owe its practical existence. Throughout the long and arduous toil, they have exhibited— allowance being made for some slight and perhaps unavoidable differences—an amount of zeal, steadiness, and intelligence which does honour to them, and to the several nations which they represent. To all—their due! If the creations of the mind stand paramount in our estimation, let appropriate honour be rendered to the skill of hand and eye, which alone can give vitality and form to our noblest conceptions. Of the advantages attendant on the erection of the Crystal Palace, even before the public are admitted to view its contents, none is more striking than the education it has already afforded to those who have taken part in its production. For the first time in England, hundreds of men have received practical instruction—in a national Fine Art School—from which society must derive a lasting benefit. It is not too much to hope that each man will act as a missionary of art and ornamental industry, in whatever quarter his improved faculties may hereafter be required.

At one time during the progress of the works as many as 6400 men were engaged in carrying out the designs of the Directors. Besides the labours already mentioned, Mr. B. Waterhouse Hawkins, in due time, took possession of a building in the grounds, and was soon busily employed, under the eye of Professor Owen, in the reproduction of those animal creations of a past age, our acquaintance with which has hitherto been confined to fossil remains. Dr. Latham was engaged in designing and giving instructions for the modelling of figures to illustrate the Ethnological department, whilst Mr. Waterhouse and Mr. Gould, aided by Mr. Thomson, as superintendent, and Mr. Bartlett, as taxidermist, were collecting and grouping valuable specimens of birds and animals to represent the science of Zoology. Towards the exhibition of the articles of industry, six architects were commissioned to erect courts for the reception of the principal manufactures of the world, and agents were employed in various parts of England, to receive the applications of intending exhibitors.

Such are a few of the operations that for the last few months have gone forward in, and in respect of, the Crystal Palace ; and, excepting by those whose business it has been to watch the progress of the works, no adequate idea can be formed of the busy activity that prevailed within the building and without, or of the marvellous manner in which the various parts of the structure seemed to grow under the hands of the workmen, until it assumed the exquisite proportions which it now possesses.

Her Majesty and his Royal Highness Prince Albert have been, from the first, graciously pleased to express their warmest sympathy with the undertaking, and have visited the Palace several times during the progress of the works. In honouring the inauguration of the Palace with her royal presence, her Majesty gives the best proof of the interest she takes in an institution which—like the great structure originated by her Royal Consort—has for its chief object the advancement of civilization and the welfare of her subjects. *

* The Queen's apartments in the Crystal Palace, destined for the reception of her Majesty and his Royal Highness Prince Albert, when they honour the Exhibition with their presence, have been erected by Messrs. J. G. Grace and Co., in the Italian style. The suite of apartments, which are placed at the north end of the building, consists of a large entrance vestibule with architectural ornaments, and painted arabesque decorations. A long corridor leads from the vestibule to the several apartments, and is formed into an arched passage by means of circular-headed doorways, before which hang *portières*, or curtains. To the right of the entrance are two rooms, one appropriated to the ladies-in-waiting, and the other to the equerries; the walls of both being divided into panels, and decorated in the Italian style. On the left are the apartments for the use of her Majesty and Prince Albert, consisting of a drawing-room and two retiring rooms. The walls of the drawing-room are divided by pilasters, the panels covered with green silk. The cove of the ceiling is decorated with arabesque ornaments.

VIEW OF PALACE FROM SECOND TERRACE.

GUIDE TO THE CRYSTAL PALACE.

THE SITE.

The Crystal Palace stands in the county of Surrey, immediately on the confines of Kent, bordered on one side by Sydenham, and on the other by Norwood and Anerley, whilst Penge lies at the foot of the hill, and Dulwich Wood at the top. No particular topographical or historical facts are associated with these places. Sydenham, however, is invested with some literary interest as having been the residence of the poet Campbell, the author of the "Pleasures of Hope," who passed, as he says in one of his letters, the happiest years of his life in this suburban village.

ENTRANCE TO THE PALACE.

The visitor, having reached the Crystal Palace terminus, quits the train, and ascends the broad flight of steps before him, leading to a covered way called the Railway Colonnade, in which will shortly be placed a collection of plants forming an avenue of choice exotics. At the end of this colonnade is the south wing of the Palace. Ascending the first flight of stairs he enters the second-class Refreshment Room, and by another flight he attains the level of the floor of the main building.*

* In the lower story of the South Wing will be found a second-class REFRESH-MENT ROOM, where refreshments of a substantial kind may be procured at a moderate charge. Above this, in the next story of the South Wing, is a first-class Refreshment Room, for confectionary and ices, as well as more nourishing fare ; and, above this again, is a large space occupying the whole of the upper floor of the Wing, and extending across the end of the main building, whilst, built out from the North end, will be found two Dining Rooms, one devoted to general use, and the other for Exhibiters only, appropriated to first-class Refreshment Tables, where cold viands may be obtained. At each end of the great Transept, under the Galleries, will be found two Stalls with ices and refreshments : and at the north end of the building, extending to the back of the Assyrian Court, and covering the top floor of the North Wing, is a large space also devoted to the sale of ices and confectionary.

Having entered the Palace, the visitor may desire, before he examines its various contents, to learn something of the Building itself—certainly not the least remarkable feature in the extraordinary scene now submitted to his contemplation. We therefore proceed at once to furnish him with an

ACCOUNT OF THE BUILDING.

In taking the structure of the Great Exhibition of 1851—that type of a class of architecture which may fairly be called "modern English " *—as the model for the new building at Sydenham, the projectors found it necessary to make such modifications and improvements as were suggested by the difference between a temporary receiving-house for the world's industrial wealth, and a permanent Palace of Art and Education, intended for the use of mankind long after its original founders should have passed away. Not only, however, have increased strength and durability been considered, but beauty and artistic effect have come in for a due share of attention. · The difference of general aspect between the present palace and its predecessor, is visible at a glance. In the parent edifice, the external appearance, although grand, was monotonous ; the long flat roof was broken by only one transept, and the want of an elevation proportionate to the great length of the building was certainly displeasing. In the Sydenham Palace, an arched roof covers the nave—raising it forty-four feet higher than the nave in Hyde Park—and three transepts are introduced into the structure instead of one, the centre transept towering into the air, and forming a hall to the Palace of surpassing brilliancy and lightness. A further improvement is the formation of recesses,

* We do not know any name more suitable to express the character of this iron and glass building than that which we have chosen. In Gothic architecture we have named one style "Early English," and we think we may with equal propriety confer the title of "Modern English" upon the new order, which is essentially the creation of the nineteenth century, and which served to house one of the greatest national displays that England ever attempted—THE GREAT EXHIBITION OF 1851. The erection of the building both of 1851 and of 1854, it may be well to remark, is mainly due to the rapid advances made in this country in the manufactures of glass and iron, substances which with only moderate attention will defy the effects of time. The present structure is capable of enduring longer than the oldest marble or stone architectural monuments of antiquity. The iron, which forms its skeleton or framework, becomes when painted, the most indestructible of materials, and the entire covering of glass may be renewed again and again without in any way interfering with the construction which it covers.

twenty-four feet deep, in the garden fronts of all the transepts. These throw fine shadows, and take away from the continuous surface of plain glass walls : whilst the whole general arrangement of the exterior—the roofs of the side aisles rising step-like to the circular roof of the nave,—the interposition of square towers at the junction of the nave and transepts,—the open galleries towards the garden front, the long wings stretching forth on either side, produce a play of light and shade, and break the building into parts, which, without in any way detracting from the grandeur and simplicity of the whole construction, or causing the parts themselves to appear mean or small, present a variety of surface that charms and fully satisfies the eye.

Unity in architecture is one of the most requisite and agreeable of its qualities : and certainly no building possesses it in a greater degree than the Crystal Palace. Its design is most simple : one portion corresponds with another ; there is no introduction of needless ornament : a simplicity of treatment reigns throughout. Nor is this unity confined to the building. It characterizes the contents of the glass structure, and prevails in the grounds. All the component parts of the Exhibition blend, yet all are distinct : and the effect of the admirable and harmonious arrangement is, that all confusion in the vast establishment, within and without, is avoided. "The mighty maze" has not only its plan, but a plan of the most lucid and instructive kind, and the visitor is enabled to examine every court, whether artistic or industrial ; every object, whether of nature or of art, in regular order ; so that, as in a well-arranged book, he may proceed from subject to subject at his discretion, and derive useful information without the trouble and vexation of working his way through a labyrinth.

All the materials employed in the Exhibition of 1851, with the exception of the glass on the whole roof, and the framing of the transept-roof, have been used in the construction of the Crystal Palace. The general principle of construction, therefore, is identical in the two buildings. The modifications that have taken place, and the reasons that have led to them, have already been stated. Two difficulties, however, which were unknown in Hyde Park, had to be provided against at Sydenham : viz., the loose nature of the soil, and the sloping character of the ground. Means were taken to overcome these difficulties at the very outset of the work. The disadvantage of soil was repaired by the introduction of masses of concrete and brickwork under each column, in order to secure breadth of base and stability of structure. The slanting ground

OPEN GALLERY TOWARDS THE GARDEN FRONT.

was seized by Sir Joseph Paxton with his usual sagacity, in order to be converted from an obstacle into a positive advantage. The ground ran rapidly down towards the garden, and Sir Joseph accordingly constructed a lower, or basement story towards the garden front, by means of which not only increased space was gained, but a higher elevation secured to the whole building, and the noblest possible view. The lower story is sufficiently large to serve as a department for the exhibition of machinery in motion, which interesting branch of science and human industry will thus be contemplated apart from other objects. Behind this space, westwards, is a capacious horizontal brick shaft, twenty-four feet wide, extending the whole length of the building, and denominated "Sir Joseph Paxton's Tunnel" (▲). Leading out of this tunnel are the furnaces and boilers connected with the heating apparatus, together with brick recesses for the stowage of coke. The tunnel itself is connected with the railway, and is used as a roadway for bringing into, and taking from, the Palace all objects of art and of industry ; an arrangement that leaves the main floor of the building independent of all such operations. Behind the tunnel, and still towards the west, the declivity of the ground is met by means of brick piers of the heights necessary to raise the foundation pieces of the columns to the level at which they rest on the summit of the hill.

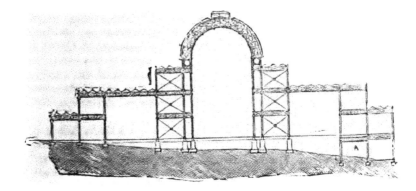

The building consists, above the basement floor, of a grand central nave, two side aisles, two main galleries, three transepts, and two wings. It will be remembered, that in Hyde Park an imposing effect was secured by the mere repetition of a column and a girder which, although striking and simple, was certainly monotonous ; and, moreover, in consequence of the great length of the building, the columns and girders succeeded one another so rapidly that the eye had no means of measuring the actual length.   At Sydenham pairs of columns and girders are advanced eight feet into the nave at every seventy-two feet, thus breaking the uniform straight line, and enabling the eye to measure and appreciate the distance.

The building above the level of the floor is entirely of iron and glass, with the exception of a portion at the north front, which is panelled with wood. The whole length of the main building is 1608 feet, and the wings 574 feet each, making a length of 2756 feet, which with the 720 feet in the colonnade, leading from the railway station to the wings, gives a total length of 3476 feet ; or nearly three-quarters of a mile of ground covered with a transparent roof of glass. The length of the Hyde Park building was 1848 feet, so that, including the wings and colonnade, the present structure is larger than its predecessor by 1628 feet ; the area of the ground floor, including the wings, amounts to the astonishing quantity of 598,396 superficial feet ; and the area of gallery flooring of building and wings to 245,260 superficial feet, altogether 843,656 superficial feet. In cubic contents the Palace at Sydenham exceeds its predecessor by nearly one-half.   The width of the nave, or main avenue, is 72 feet, which is also the width of the north and south transepts ; and the height of all three from the floor to the springing or base of the arch, is 68 feet; the height from the flooring to the crown or top of the arch being 104 feet, just the height of the transept at the old building.   The length of the north and south transepts, is 336 feet respectively.   The length of the central transept is 384 feet ; its width 120 feet; its height from the floor to the top of the louvre, or ventilator, 168 feet ; from the floor to the springing of the arch, 108 feet ; and from the garden front to the top of the louvre, 208 feet, or 6 feet higher than the Monument.

The floor consists of boarding one inch and a half thick, laid as in the old building, with half-inch openings between them, and resting on joists, placed two feet apart, seven inches by two and a half inches thick.   These joists are carried on sleepers and props eight feet apart.   The girders which support the galleries and the roof-work, and carry the brick arches over the basement floor, are of cast-iron, and are 24 feet in length.   The connexions between the girders and columns are applied in the same manner as in the building of 1851.   The principle of connexion was originally condemned by some men of standing in the scientific world ; but experience has proved it to be sound and admirable in every respect. The mode of connexion is not merely that of resting the girders on the columns in order to support the roofs and galleries, but the top and bottom of each girder are firmly secured to each of the columns, so that the girder preserves the perpendicularity of the column, and secures lateral stiffness to the entire edifice. Throughout the building the visitor will notice, at certain intervals, diagonally placed, rods connected at the crossing, and uniting column with column. These are the diagonal bracings, or the rods provided to resist the action of the wind : they are strong enough to bear any strain that can be brought to bear against them, and are fitted with screwed connexions and couplings, so that they can be adjusted with the greatest accuracy. The roof, from end to end, is on the Paxton ridge-and-furrow system, and the glass employed in the roof is $\frac{1}{13}$ of an inch in thickness (21 oz. per foot). The discharge of the rain-water is effected by gutters, from which the water is conveyed down the inside of the columns, at the base of which are the necessary outlets leading to the main-drains of the building. The first gallery is gained from the ground-floor by means of a flight of stairs about 23 feet high ; eight such flights being distributed over the building. This gallery is 24 feet wide, and devoted to the exhibition of articles of industry. The upper gallery is 8 feet wide, extending, like the other, round the building ; it is gained from the lower gallery, by spiral staircases, of which there are ten : each stair-case being divided into two flights, and each flight being 20 feet high. Round this upper gallery, at the very summit of the nave and transepts, as well as round the ground floor of the building, are placed louvres, or ventilators, made of galvanized iron. By the opening or closing of these louvres—a service readily performed—the temperature of the Crystal Palace is so regulated that on the hottest day of summer, the dry parching heat mounts to the roof to be dismissed, whilst a pure and invigorating supply is introduced at the floor in its place, giving new life to the thirsty plant and fresh vigour to man. The coolness thus obtained within the palace will be sought in vain on such a summer's day outside the edifice.

The total length of columns employed in the construction of the main buildings and wings would extend, if laid in a straight line, to a distance of sixteen miles and a quarter. The total weight of iron used in the main building and wings amounts to 9,641 tons, 17 cwts., 1 quarter. The superficial quantity of glass used is 25

acres ; and, if the panes were laid side by side, they would extend
to a distance of 48 miles ; if end to end, to the almost incredible
length of 242 miles.   To complete our statistics, we have further
to add that the quantity of bolts and rivets distributed over the
main structure and wings weighs 175 tons, 1 cwt., 1 quarter ;
that the nails hammered into, the Palace increase its weight by
103 tons, 6 cwt., and that the amount of brick-work in the main
building and wings is 15391 cubic yards.

From the end of the south wing to the Crystal Palace Railway-
station, as above indicated, is a colonnade 720 feet long, 17
feet wide, and 18 feet high.   It possesses a superficial area of
15,500 feet, and the quantity of iron employed in this covered
passage is 60 tons ; of glass 30,000 superficial feet.

HOT-WATER APPARATUS.

Vast as are the proportions of the Crystal Palace, novel and
scientific as is the principle of construction, we are in some degree
prepared for this magnificent result of intellect and industry by
the Great Exhibition of 1851.   One arrangement, however,
in the present structure, admits of no comparison ; for, in
point of extent, it leaves all former efforts in the same direction
far behind, and stands by itself unrivalled.   We refer to the
process of warming the atmosphere in the enormous Glass Palace
to the mild and genial heat of Madeira, throughout our cold and
damp English winter.

The employment of hot water as a medium for heating apartments, seems to have been first hinted at in the year 1594, by Sir
Hugh Platt, who, in a work entitled "The Jewell House of
Art and Nature," published in that year, suggests the use of hot
water as a safe means of drying gunpowder, and likewise
recommends it for heating a plant-house.   In 1716, Sir
Martin Triewald of Newcastle-on-Tyne, proposed a scheme for
heating a green-house by hot water ; and a Frenchman, M. Bonnemain, a short time afterwards invented an apparatus for hatching
chickens by the same means.   In the early part of this century
Sir Martin Triewald's plan of heating was applied to conservatories,
at St. Petersburgh ; and a few years later, Bonnemain's arrangement
was introduced into England, where it has undergone several
improvements, and occupied the attention of scientific men.
Its application to the heating of churches, public libraries, and
other buildings, has been attended with considerable success, and

it is now looked upon as the safest, as well as one of the most effectual artificial methods of heating.

The simple plan of heating by hot water is that which Sir Joseph Paxton has adopted for the Crystal Palace. But simple as the method undoubtedly is, its adaptation to the purposes of the Palace has cost infinite labour and anxious consideration : for hitherto it has remained an unsolved problem how far, and in what quantity, water could be made to travel through pipes—flowing and returning by means of the propulsion of heat from the boilers. At Chatsworth, the seat of the Duke of Devonshire, the principle has been carried out on a large scale, and the experiment there tried has yielded data and proof : but in the present building, a greater extent of piping has been attached to the boilers than was ever before known, or even contemplated. In order to give the visitor some idea of the magnitude of the operation in question, it will be sufficient to state that the pipes for the conveyance of the hot water, laid under the floor of the main building, and around the wings, would, if placed in a straight line, and taken at an average circumference of 12 inches, stretch to a distance of more than 50 miles, and that the water in flowing from and returning to the boilers, travels one mile and three-quarters. But even with these extraordinary results obtained, the question as to the distance to which water can be propelled by means of heat, is far from being definitely settled. Indeed, Sir Joseph Paxton and Mr. Henderson have invented an ingenious contrivance, by means of which, should it ever be required, a much larger heating surface may be called forth at any time in any particular portion of the building.

The general arrangement of the Heating Apparatus may be described as follows :—Nearly twenty-four feet below the surface of the flooring of the main building, and leading out of " Sir Joseph Paxton's tunnel " * (the name given to the roadway in the

---

* The formation of tunnels, for the passage of water especially, and for drainage, was well known to the ancient Greeks and Romans, and the remains of many of their great works of this kind possess an extreme interest. In the tunnel or underground canal of the Abruzzi in Italy, formed by the Roman Emperor Claudius, and lately cleared out by the Neapolitan Government, nearly the same means appear to have been used for its excavation and construction as are employed in forming tunnels at the present day. Amongst other remarkable tunnels of antiquity may be cited that of Posilipo at Naples, nearly three-quarters of a mile long, probably constructed about the time of Tiberius (circa A.D. 30), and the Greek tunnel, 4200 Greek feet in length, excavated through a mountain for the purpose of conveying water to the city of Samos. One of the earliest tunnels of modern times was made at Languedoc in

basement story, extending the whole length of the building on the side nearest the Gardens), are placed, at certain intervals, boiler-houses, each containing two boilers capable of holding 11,000 gallons of water. The boilers are twenty-two in number, and are set in pairs. In addition to these, a boiler is placed at the north end of the building, on account of the increased heat there required for the tropical plants. There are also two boilers set in the lower stories of each wing, and two small boilers are appropriated to the water in the fountain basins at each end of the building, which contain Victoria Regias and other aquatic plants of tropical climes. Four pipes are immediately connected with each boiler ; two of such pipes convey the water from the boiler, and the other two bring it back ; they are called the main pipes, and are nine inches in diameter.

Of the two pipes that convey the water from the boiler, one crosses the building transversely—from the garden-front to the opposite side. Connected with this pipe, at certain distances, and in allotted numbers, are smaller pipes, five inches in diameter, laid horizontally, and immediately beneath the flooring of the building. These convey the water from the main pipe to certain required distances, and then bring it back to the *return* main pipe, through which it flows into the boiler. The second main pipe conveys the water for heating the front of the building next to the Garden ; and connected with this, as with the other main pipe, are smaller pipes through which the water ramifies, and then, in like manner, is returned to the boiler. Thus, then, by the mere propulsion of heat, a vast quantity of water is kept in constant motion throughout the Palace, continually flowing and returning, and giving out warmth that makes its way upwards, and disseminates a genial atmosphere in every part.

To ensure pure circulation throughout the winter, ventilators have been introduced direct from the main building into each furnace, where the air, so brought, being consumed by the fire, the atmosphere in the Palace is continually renewed.

THE ARTESIAN WELL, AND THE SUPPLY OF THE FOUNTAINS.

In July, 1852, the supply of water for the fountains and other great works in connexion with the Crystal Palace, first seriously

France, A.D. 1666 : since that period they have become general. The great labour required in their formation, is likely to be obviated by the invention of a machine by an American, which is said to be capable of cutting a rapid way even through masses of rock.

engaged the attention of the Directors.   Various proposals were
made, and suggestions offered: some were at once rejected: others,
although not free from difficulties, were taken into consideration.
The most feasible of these was that which involved the extension
to Sydenham of the pipes of one of the nearest London water-
work companies,—a measure that would at once secure a sufficient
supply of tolerably good water. Against the proposition for sinking
a well on the grounds, it was urged that the neighbourhood is
almost destitute of water ; that wells already excavated to the
depth of two hundred feet had yielded but a small supply ; and
that even if a sufficient supply could be secured by digging, the
water obtained could never be raised to the top of the hill.

Acting, however, upon sound advice, and after due consideration,
the company commenced the sinking of an artesian well at the foot
of the hill on which the Palace stands, and after proceeding to a
depth of 250 feet, their efforts were rewarded.   They have now
carried the well down 570 feet from the surface, and require only
time to complete their operations and to secure water sufficient for
their novel and interesting displays.

When an abundant supply of water shall have been brought to
the foot of the hill, it will be necessary not only to raise it to the
top, on a level with the building, but also to elevate it to a sufficient height for obtaining the fall requisite for fountains to throw up
water to a height varying from 70 to 250 feet. The following is a brief
outline of the arrangements now making to effect these objects :—

Three reservoirs have been formed at different levels in the
grounds, the lowest one being on the same level as the largest
basins placed nearly at the base of the hill ; the second, or intermediate reservoir, is higher up, and in a line with the basin in the
central walk ; whilst the third, or upper reservoir, stands on the
top of the hill immediately adjoining the north end of the building.
Next to the Artesian Well, a small engine is placed which raises
the water required to be permanently maintained in the reservoirs
and in the basins of the fountains, and which will subsequently
supply, or keep up the water that is lost by waste and evaporation.

The reservoir on the summit of the hill contains the water
required for the use of the building, and for the fountains
throughout the grounds.   Close to this reservoir is an engine-
house, containing the steam-engines that raise part of the water in
the reservoir into two large tanks (each capable of holding
200,000 gallons of water), placed at the summit of the square
towers terminating the wings. From these towers the water

D

flows to the basins in the grounds, and there throws up jets of 70 to 120 feet in height. These engines likewise lift to a proper elevation the water necessary for the interior of the building, and for making proper provision against fire. The remainder of the water in the top reservoir, in consequence of the sloping character of the ground, will not need any help from the engines, but will flow direct to fountains on a lower level, and play smaller jets. Through the same convenience, the waste water from the upper fountains will be used a second time in the lower fountains.

The centre or intermediate reservoir collects the waste water from the displays which take place on ordinary days, and which will include all the fountains save the two largest and the cascades. Attached to this reservoir are also engines which pump the water back to the upper reservoir. The lowest reservoir collects similarly the waste water from the displays which will be presented in the two largest fountains on the days of great exhibition, and its engines will return the water at once to the top level. With the exception of the two largest fountains, which cannot play until the towers, which have to supply jets of 250 feet high, are built at each end of the building, the water-works of the Palace will shortly be complete in every respect.

From the above simple statement it will be seen, that the arrangements for supplying the fountains with water are at once simple, complete, and based upon the most economical principles. The engine power employed is that of three hundred and twenty horses ; the water itself is conveyed to and from the reservoirs in pipes varying from three feet to one inch in diameter ; and the weight of piping may be set down at 4000 tons, its length, roughly estimated, at ten miles.

The name Artesian is derived from the province of Artois in France, where it is supposed that these wells were first constructed, although it has been asserted that they were sunk in Italy at an earlier period, and that they were even in use amongst the ancients. An Artesian well may be briefly described as a small boring or sinking in the ground through which water rises to, or nearly to, the surface of the earth, in compliance with that well known law which causes water to seek its level.

In the present case, the water which appears in the well comes from a reservoir lying between the London clay and the hard under-rocks as its upper and lower envelopes. This reservoir is supplied by rain water, which, percolating the porous superficial and upper strata, and finding an impediment to its downward progress on reaching the rocks, flows transversely into the space between the hard clay and rock, as into a cistern. The process by which the reservoir is supplied is continuous, the water finding its way down to it as if by a series of small tubes, and pressing against the lower surface of the clay with a force which, if unresisted, would raise it to the level from which it descended. When the clay is pierced by the auger it is evident that this force is free to act, the resistance of the clay at the point where it is pierced being removed, and accordingly the water rises in the bore to the level from which it is supplied, and will continue to do so as long as the percolation lasts. The most remarkable Artesian well yet made is one at Kissingen in Bavaria, which, in 1852, reached a depth of 2000 feet. As a commercial speculation it has been attended with complete success. The water is saline. *

THE NAVE.

Quitting the wing, to which the visitor was brought, he turns into the body of the Palace, and the first object that attracts attention is a fountain of toilet vinegar, erected by Mr. E. Rimmel, from designs furnished by Mr. John Thomas. Keeping close to this, the south end of the Palace, we proceed towards the centre of the nave, and passing through the opening in the ornamental screen which stretches across the nave, a fine view is gained of the whole interior of the building. In the fore-ground is Osler's crystal fountain, which adorned the Palace in Hyde Park, but here elevated in its proportions and improved. It is surrounded by a sheet of water at each end of which float the gigantic leaves of the Victoria Regia, the intermediate space being occupied by various aquatic plants ; several species of the Nymphœa Devoniana, the Nelumbium speciosum or sacred bean of the Pythagoreans, &c. On either side of the nave the plants of almost every clime wave their foliage, forming a mass of cool pleasant colour, admirably

* Fountains were well known to the ancient Greeks and Romans, who ornamented their cities with them. It would appear that the latter were acquainted with the law by which water ascends from a jet ; painted representations of such fountains having been found at Pompeii. The discovery is attributed to Hero of Alexandria, about 150 B.C. However this may be, the law itself was never applied in practice to any extent. The next jet-fountain we meet with is on the celebrated mosaic work at San Vitale, Ravenna, about 530 A.D. We are not aware of any examples of jet-fountains occurring amongst Europeans or Orientals of the middle ages, though ordinary fountains were plentiful. The great jets of comparatively modern fountains are the result of our advanced scientific knowledge.

harmonizing with the surrounding tints, and also acting as a most effective background to relieve the white ˛ statues, which are picturesquely grouped along the nave ; at the back of these are the façades of the various Industrial and Fine-Art Courts, whose bright colouring gives additional brilliancy to the interior, whilst the aërial blue tint of the arched roof above considerably increases the effect of the whole composition.

Let the visitor now proceed up the building until he arrives at the central transept, at which point he will be enabled to judge of the vastness of the hall in the midst of which he stands, and of the whole structure of which the transept forms so noble and conspicuous a part.

THE GREAT TRANSEPT.

Immediately on his right in the transept is a selection of works of the old school of French Sculptors in front of the Gallery of French Portraits, which commences immediately behind the statue of Admiral Duquesne. On the opposite corresponding side are ranged the works of Canova, behind which, commencing near the statue of Rubens, is placed the Italian portion of the Portrait Gallery. On the left is a selection from the works of English Sculptors, at the back of which are ranged the German portraits, commencing at the Statue of Peel by Marochetti. On the north-west side of the transept are selections from the ancient Roman and Greek Schools of Sculpture, fronting the English portraits which begin at the back of the statue of the Farnese Hercules. The schools of French and Italian sculpture, and of German and English sculpture were passed by the visitor at the junction of the nave and transept. Corresponding to these courts, at the junction on the opposite side, are Courts of the Gothic and Renaissance, and of Greek and Roman sculpture. Full accounts of all the works of art that attract and seize the eye of the visitor at this point will be found in the Handbooks that deal especially with these subjects. When a sufficient idea of this portion of the Building has been obtained, he will do well to pass at once towards the architectural restorations which await him on the other side of the transept.

In order the better to appreciate the arrangement of those restorations through which we now propose to conduct the visitor, a few words explanatory of the object which they are intended to serve may prove of use.

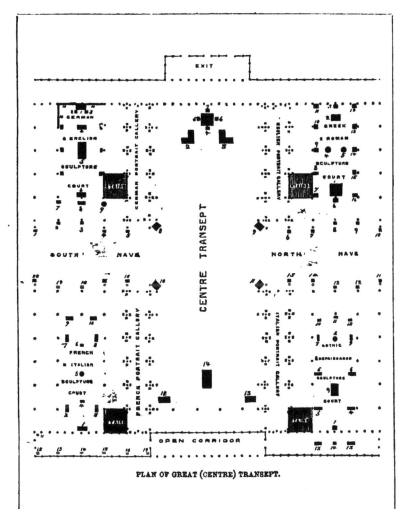

PLAN OF GREAT (CENTRE) TRANSEPT.

NORTH NAVE.	SOUTH NAVE.
Greek and Roman Sculpture Court.	German and English Sculpture Court.
English Portrait Gallery.	German Portrait Gallery.
Gothic and Renaissance Sculpture Court.	French and Italian Sculpture Court.
Italian Portrait Gallery.	French Portrait Gallery.

Olympian Jupiter.

INTRODUCTION TO THE FINE ARTS COURTS.

ONE of the most important objects of the Crystal Palace is to teach a great practical lesson in art. Specimens of the various phases through which the arts of Architecture and Sculpture have passed, are here collected, commencing from the earliest known period down to modern times, or from the remote ages of Egyptian civilization to the sixteenth century after Christ—a period of more than three thousand years.

Perhaps no subject, with the exception of the literature of departed nations, affords more interest to the mind of man, than these visible proofs of the different states of society throughout the world's history; and nothing better aids us in realizing the people and customs of the past, than the wonderful monuments happily preserved from the destructive hand of Time, and now restored to something of their original splendour by the patient and laborious researches of modern times; and, we may add, (not without some pride) by the enterprising liberality of Englishmen.

Nor is it the least extraordinary fact, in this view of progress, that the building itself, which contains these valuable monuments of past ages, is essentially different from every preceding style, uniting perfect strength with aërial lightness, and as easy of erection as it is capable of endurance. The combination of glass and iron has produced the original and beautiful result of which the Crystal Palace is the most brilliant example, suggesting to the mind a new and wonderful power of extension beyond anything the mind of the artist has yet devised. Thus then, beneath one roof, may the visitor trace the course of art from centuries long anterior to Christianity, down to the very moment in which he lives, and obtain by this means an idea of the successive states of civilization which from time to time have arisen in the world, flourishing for a greater or less period, until overturned by the aggressions of barbarians, or the no less destructive agency of a sensual and degraded luxury. Sculpture, the sister art of architecture, has also been worthily illustrated within our walls. Vainly, in any part of the world, will be sought a similar collection, by means of which the progress of that beautiful art can be regularly traced.

The statues will generally be found in the Architectural Courts of the countries to which they belong, so that the eye may track the intellectual stream as it flows on, now rising to the highest point of beauty, and now sinking to the lowest depths of degradation. The visitor is invited to proceed with us on this world-wide tour of inspection, but to bear also in mind that our present task is to show him how to see the Building itself, and not to describe its contents, except by briefly pointing out the most remarkable objects that encounter him on his way. For detailed and valuable information the visitor is referred to the excellent Handbooks of the respective Courts, all of which describe with minuteness not only their contents, but every needful circumstance in connexion with their history. The point from which we start is the central transept. Proceeding northwards, up the nave, the visitor turns immediately to the left and finds himself in front of

THE EGYPTIAN COURT.

The remains of Egyptian Architecture are the most ancient yet discovered. They possess an absorbing interest, not only on account of the connexion of Egypt with Biblical history, but also of the perfect state of the remains, which enable us to judge of the high state of civilization to which Egypt attained, and which have permitted the decipherers of the hieroglyphics, led by Dr. Young, Champollion, and Sir Gardner Wilkinson, in our own time, to give us clear insight into the manner of life —public and private—of this early and interesting nation.

Egyptian architecture is characterized by simplicity of construction, gigantic proportions, and massive solidity. The buildings were almost entirely of stone, and many of them are excavations and shapings of rocks. The examples of this architecture now before us are not taken from any one ruin, but are illustrations of various styles, commencing with the earliest, and terminating with the latest, so that we are enabled to follow the gradual development of the art. Little change, however, was effected during its progress. The original solidity so admirably suited to the requirements of the Egyptians continued to the end; and religion forbade a change in the conventional representations of those gods and kings which so extensively cover the temples and tombs. So that we find the same peculiar character continued in a great measure to the very last.

Advancing up the avenue of lions, cast from a pair brought from Egypt by Lord Prudhoe (the present Duke of Northumberland), we have before us the outer walls and columns of a temple, not taken from any one particular structure, but composed from various sources, to illustrate Egyptian columns and capitals during the Ptolemaic period, somewhere about 300 years B.C. On the walls are coloured sunk-reliefs showing a king making offerings or receiving gifts from the gods. The capitals or heads of the columns are palm- and lotus-leaved; some showing the papyrus in its various stages of development, from the simple bud to the full-blown flower. The representation of the palm and the papyrus occurs frequently in Egyptian architecture; the leaves of the latter, it will be remembered, were made into paper, and its flowers were specially used as offerings in the temples. On the frieze above the columns is a hieroglyphic inscription stating that "in the seventeenth year of the reign of Victoria, the ruler of the waves, this Palace was erected and furnished with a thousand statues, a thousand plants, &c., like as a book for the use of the men of all countries." This inscription is repeated, with some slight additions, on the frieze of the interior of the Court. On the cornice of both the inside and outside of the Court, are the names of Her Majesty and Prince Albert, engraved in hieroglyphic characters, and also winged globes, the symbolic protecting deity of doorways. Entering by the central doorway, on the lintels and sides of which are inserted the different titles of King Ptolemy in hieroglyphics, we find ourselves in the exterior court of a temple in which the multitude assembled; the decorations of the walls are similar to those we saw outside, and it must be borne in mind that the colouring is taken from actual remains in Egypt.   On the wall to the left is a large picture copied from the great Temple of Rameses III. or Rameses Mai Amun, at Medinet Haboo near Thebes, showing the counting of the hands of the slain before the king who is in his chariot ; on the right hand side of the Court is a representation of a battle-scene, with the Egyptians storming a fortress.   Turning to the left, after examining the eight gigantic figures of Rameses the Great, forming the façade of another temple,

The Gigantic Figures of Rameses the Great.

we enter the colonnade of an early period, its date being about 1300 B.C.   The columns represent eight stems and buds of the papyrus bound together, and are cast from a black granite column bearing the name of Amunoph, now in the British Museum.

Passing on we find ourselves in a dark tomb copied from one at Beni Hassan.   It is the earliest piece of architecture in the Crystal Palace, its date being about 1660, B.C.   The original tomb is cut in the solid chain of rocks that forms a boundary on the east of the Nile, separating the sandy desert from the fertile valley of the river.   Although architectural remains exist in Egypt of a much earlier date than this tomb, it still possesses great value to us, for it may be considered as exhibiting the first *order* of Egyptian columns, which was employed in constructing buildings at as remote a period as two thousand years before Christ ; this fluted column in another respect claims our attention, for there can be but little doubt that it supplied the Greeks with the model of their early Doric.

Passing out, we behold, in front of us, a beautiful colonnade, from the Island of Philœ, and of the same period as the

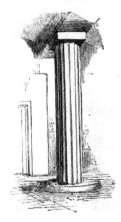

Egyptian wall which we first saw fronting the nave. Within this Court we cannot fail to remark the scattered statues, especially the Egyptian Antinous, executed during the Roman rule, the life-like development of whose limbs, representing, as it no doubt does, the Egyptian type, is sufficient to convince us that when Egyptian art was not tied down by the hierarchical yoke, it was capable of producing works of truth and merit. Amidst the statues will be found two circular-headed stones—copies of the celebrated Rosetta stone (so called from having been found at the little town of Rosetta, near Alexandria) from which Dr. Young and Champollion obtained a key to the deciphering of hieroglyphics. The

First order of Egyptian Column.

stone is engraved in three characters : Hieroglyphics, Enchorial—the writing of the country—and Greek; the inscription is an address from the priests to the Greek King of Egypt, Ptolemy V., in which the sovereign's praises are set forth, and orders are given to set up a statue of the king, together with the address, in every temple. The date of this interesting remnant of Egyptian manners and customs is about 200 years before the Christian era. Further on to the right—in a recess, is the model of the temple of Aboo Simbel, cut in the side of a rock, in Nubia. The sitting figures represent Rameses the Great, and the smaller ones around, his mother, wife, and daughter. The original tomb is ten times as large as the present model. Some notion of the stupendous magnitude of these Egyptian remains may be formed by observing the small figure standing on the tomb, which shows the relative height of an ordinary living man. Turning from this recess, and after looking at the beautiful lotus columns to the left, surmounted by the cow-eared Goddess of Love of the Egyptians, and having examined the two large pictures on the walls of the temple—one of which represents a king slaying his enemies with the aid of the god Ammon Ra, and the other a feat of arms of the same king—

TOMB OF BENI HASSAN.

we direct our attention to the columns before us, which are reduced models of a portion of the celebrated Temple of Karnac at Thebes. This temple was, perhaps, one of the largest and most interesting in Egypt ; the principal portions said to have been erected by Rameses II. about 1170 B. C. It seems to have been a fashion with the Theban kings to make additions to this temple during their respective reigns ; and, as each monarch was anxious to outvie his predecessor, the size of the fabric threatened to become unbounded. Temples and tombs were the grand extravagances of the Egyptian kings. The sums that modern rulers devote to palaces which add to their splendour whilst living, were given by the remote princes of whom we speak, and who regarded life as only a fleet passage towards eternity, for the construction of enduring homes when life should have passed away. Inasmuch as, if the career of an Egyptian king proved irreligious or oppressive, the priests and people could deny him sepulture in his own tomb, it is not unlikely that many Egyptian kings lavished large sums upon temples, in order to conciliate the priestly favour, and to secure for their embalmed bodies the much-prized sanctuary.

It is to be observed, however, with respect to the names and inscriptions found on Egyptian monuments, that they are by no means always to be taken as an authentic account of the illustrious remains within. Some of the Egyptian kings have been proved guilty of erasing from tombs the names of their predecessors, and of substituting their own ; an unwarrantable and startling deception that has proved very awkward and embarrassing to Egyptian antiquaries.

The portion of Karnac here modelled is taken from the Hall of Columns, commenced by Osirei the First, and completed by his son, Rameses the Great—a most illustrious monarch, who flourished during the

Column from Karnac.

twelfth century before Christ, whose deeds are frequently recorded, and whose statue is found in many parts of Egypt. Before entering the temple we stay to notice the representations of animals and birds on the frieze above the columns, which is the dedication of the temple to the gods. Entering between the columns, on the lower part of which is the name of Rameses the Great, and, in the middle, a representation of the three principal divinities of Thebes receiving offerings from King Osirei ;—and, after thoroughly examining this interesting restoration, we return again into the outer court. Regaining the nave, a few steps, directed to the left, bring us to

The Parthenon.

THE GREEK COURT.

Architecture and sculpture have here made a stride. We have noted even in Egypt the advance from early rude effort to a consistent gigantic system of art, that covers and almost darkens the land under the shadow of a stern hierarchical religion. We step at once from the gloom into the sunshine of Greek art. The overwhelming grandeur of Egypt, with its austere conventionalities is exchanged for true simplicity, great beauty, and ideality. Just proportions, truth, and grace of form and appropriate ornament characterized Greek architecture. The fundamental principles of construction, as will readily be seen, were the same in Greece as in Egypt, but improved, added to, and perfected. The architecture of both countries was columnar ;. but, compare the Greek columns before us with those which we just now saw in Egypt, taken from the tomb of Beni Hassan ; the latter are simple, rude, ill-proportioned, and with slight pretension to beauty, whilst, in the former, the simplicity still prevailing, the rudeness and heaviness have departed, the pillars taper gracefully, and are finely proportioned and elegant, though of great strength. The specimen of Greek architecture before us is from the later period of the first order, namely, the Doric; and the court is taken, in part, from the Temple of Jupiter at Nemea, which was built about 400 years B.C., still within the verge of the highest period of Greek Art, Passing along the front, we notice on the frieze above the columns the names of the principal Greek cities and colonies.

We enter the court through the central opening. This portion represents part of a Greek *agora*, or forum, which was used as a market, and also for public festivals, for political and other assemblies. Around the frieze in this central division are the names of the poets, artists, philosophers of Greece, and of their most celebrated patrons, the list commencing immediately above the place of entrance, with old blind Homer, and finishing with Anthemius the architect of Saint Sophia at Constantinople. The names, it will be remarked, are inserted in the Greek characters of the period at which the various persons lived. The monograms within the chaplets on the frieze are formed of the initial letters of the Muses, the Graces, the Good and the Wise; on the walls are also pictures representing the Olympian Gods and Marriage of Peleus and Thetis, the Judgment of Paris, Destruction of Ilium, and Escape of Æneas and Anchises, Hades and the Argonautic expedition. The colouring of this court, with its blue, red, and yellow surfaces, blazoned with gold, produces an excellent effect. It is the object of the decorators to give to the whole of the architectural specimens in the Crystal Palace, those colours which there is reason to know, or to believe, they originally possessed; to restore them, in fact, as far as possible to their pristine state, in order that the imagination of the spectator may be safely conducted back in contemplation to the artistic characteristics of distant and distinctive ages. In this court are arranged sculptures and models of temples. Amongst the former will be recognised many of the finest statues and groups of the Greek school, the Laocoon (16); the Farnese Juno (6); the well-known Discobolus (4) from the Vatican; the Ariadne, also from the Vatican (27); the Sleeping, or Barberini Faun (19); and, in the centre, the unrivalled Venus of Melos (1).* We make our way round this court, beginning at the right hand. After examining the collection, we pass between the columns into the small side court, (next to Egypt), answering to a stoa of the Agora. Around the frieze are

* These numbers refer to the Handbook of the Greek Court.

found the names of the great men of the Greek colonies, arranged in chronological order. The visitor has here an opportunity of contrasting the architecture and sculpture of the Egyptians with those of the Greeks. On one side of him is an Egyptian wall inclining inwards, with its angular pictorial decorations, and the passive colossal figures guarding the entrances. On the other side are the beautiful columns and bold cornice of the Greek Doric, surrounded by statues characterized by beauty of form and refined idealized expression. In this division will also be found the busts of the Greek Poets, arranged in chronological order, commencing on the right-hand side from the nave : these form a portion of the Portrait Gallery of the Crystal Palace.

Portrait of Homer.

Making our way through the opening in the back, opposite the Nave, we enter a covered atrium, commonly attached to the portion of the agora here reproduced. The massive *antæ*, or square pillars, and the panelled ceiling —the form of the latter adapted from the Temple of Apollo at Bassæ in Arcadia — give the visitor another specimen of Greek architecture. We proceed, to the right, down this atrium, occasionally stepping out to examine the sculpture arranged in the gallery, and the restored and coloured frieze of the Parthenon of Athens, which extends its length along the wall. The coloured portion has been executed under the direction of Mr. Owen Jones, the golden hair and the several tints being founded on authentic examples which still exist on analogous remains of ancient Greek art. This frieze represents the Panathenaic procession to the temple of Athene Polias, which formed part of the display at this greatest of the Athenian festivals, and took place every fourth year. Dividing the frieze, is one of the most interesting objects in the Crystal Palace, a model of the western front of the Parthenon itself, about one-fourth the size of the original structure. This is the largest model that has ever been constructed of this beautiful temple, and, being coloured from actual remains and legitimate deductions, it possesses the great charm of a veritable copy. The scale is sufficiently large to give a complete idea of the original. This admirable model is due to the intelligent and successful researches prosecuted in Athens by Mr. Penrose, whose labours have thrown so much new light upon the refinements practised by the Greeks in architecture. Mr. Penrose has himself directed the construction of the model. In this gallery are ranged statues and groups, including the celebrated Niobe group, from Florence (187 to 187 L, inclusive). This subject of the punishment of Niobe's family by the gods was frequently treated by Greek artists ; and certainly the group before us is one of the most beautiful examples of Greek sculptural art. It is supposed that the portion of the group at Florence occupied the pediment of the temple of Apollo Sosianus at Rome. The Niobe group belongs to one of the brightest periods. Casts from those most beautiful and wonderful remains of ancient art, the colossal figures from the pediment of the Parthenon at Athens, are also here (185 to 185 B.). The originals, brought over to England by Lord Elgin in 1801-2, are in the British Museum, and the nation is indebted for the acquisition to the painter Haydon, who was the first British artist to recognise the value, and appreciate the beauty of these mutilated but inimitable monuments of art at the highest period of its glory. They belong to the Phidian school, and are characterized by simple grandeur, great repose in the attitudes, and a deep study of nature in their forms. The Theseus more particularly displays a marvellous study and appreciation of nature. In connexion with the Parthenon will also be seen a cast from a part of one of the actual columns, also in the British Museum (150).* In this Stoa is the wonderful Belvedere Torso, from the Vatican (67); the far-famed Venus de' Medici (198), from Florence, and the exquisite Psyche (199), from the Museum at Naples. The visitor will not fail to be astonished, no less by the number than by the charming effect of these works which have come down to our time, and which will descend to the latest posterity as models of excellence. Proceeding until we arrive at the junction of the Greek and Roman Courts, we turn into the right hand division of the outer court ; round the frieze of which are the names of the statesmen and warriors of Athens, the Peloponnesus and

---

* For a minute description of all the statues and other works of art in this Court, see the "Handbook to the Greek Court."

Attica. The busts ranged on either side are portraits of the Greek philosophers, orators, generals and statesmen, arranged in chronological order, commencing at the entrance from the nave.

GREEK SCULPTURES.

No.
1. VENUS VICTRIX.
2. VENUS VICTRIX OF CAPUA.
3. DIONE.
4. QUOIT-THROWER.
5. THE WARRIOR OF AGASIAS.
6. JUNO.
7. NAIAD.
8. APOLLO.
9. MERCURY.
10. FAUN.
11. COLOSSAL FEMALE FIGURE.
12. FAUN.
13. SCYTHIAN.
14. DANAID.
15. VACANT.
16. LAOCOON AND HIS SONS.
17. FARNESE MINERVA.
18. MINERVA.
19. SLEEPING FAUN.
20. YOUTH.
21. JASON.
22. DIANA.
23. LUDOVISI MARS.
24. GENIUS OF DEATH.
25. JASON.
26. APOLLO LYCIUS.
27. ARIADNE.
28. MINERVA.
29. MINERVA.
30. SOMNUS.
31. CLIO.
32. FRIEZE IN ALTO-RILIEVO.
33. ENDYMION.
34. BAS-RELIEF.
35. PERSEUS AND ANDROMEDA.
36. POLYHYMNIA.
37. MINERVA.
38 & 39. CANEPHORÆ.
40. MINERVA.
41. FLORA.
42. HYGIEIA.
43. SMALL STATUE OF FEMALE.
44. EUTERPE.
45. VESTA.
46. EUTERPE.
47. BORGHESE FLORA.
48. MINERVA.
49. A MUSE.
50. POLYHYMNIA.
51. THALIA.
52. A BRONZE FIGURE.
53. TORSO OF AN AMAZON.
54. MINERVA.
55. SMALL FEMALE FIGURE.
56. THE EAST FRIEZE OF THE THESEUM.
57. PORTION OF FRIEZE.
58. BATTLE OF THE AMAZONS.
59. BAS-RELIEF.
60. MINERVA.

No.
61. PUTEAL.
62. TORSO OF A FAUN.
63. ÆSCULAPIUS AND TELESPHORUS.
64. POMONA.
65. PHILOSOPHER.
66. TORSO OF A YOUTHFUL MALE FIGURE.
67. A SEATED HERCULES.
68. TORSO OF A FEMALE FIGURE.
69. HORSE'S HEAD.
70. POLYHYMNIA.
71. HORSE'S HEAD.
72. TORSO AND LEGS OF A DELICATELY FORMED FEMALE.
73. MARSYAS.
74. HORSE'S HEAD.
75. DIANA.
76. ANTINOUS AND HIS GENIUS WITH SMALL STATUE OF ELPIS.
77. GANYMEDES AND EAGLE.
78. CUPID AND PSYCHE.
79. THALIA.
80. AUGUSTUS.
81. APOLLO.
82. CERES.
83. BACCHUS CROWNED WITH IVY.
84. VICTORY.
85. PENELOPE AND TELEMACHUS.
86. HALF-DRAPED FEMALE STATUE.
87. THETIS.
88. GANYMEDES.
89. BACCHUS.
90. ÆSCULAPIUS.
91. HUNTER.
92. JULIAN THE APOSTATE.
93. ARCHITECTURAL SCROLLWORK.
94. ARCHITECTURAL SCROLLWORK.
95. ARCHITECTURAL ORNAMENT.
96 & 98. TWO PORTIONS OF A FRIEZE.
97. SPAIN.
99. ARCHITECTURAL ORNAMENT OF A GRIFFIN.
100. BOLD ARCHITECTURAL ORNAMENTS.
101. ARCHITECTURAL SCROLLWORK.
102. ARCHITECTURAL SCROLLWORK.
103. ARCHITECTURAL FRAGMENT.
104. ARCHITECTURAL FRET.
105. ARCHITECTURAL PORTIONS OF A CORNICE.
106—110. ARCHITECTURAL FRAGMENTS.
111. LARGE LION'S HEAD.
112. CAPITAL.
113—116. ARCHITECTURAL FRAGMENTS.
117. LUCILLA.
118. THE FRONT OF A LARGE SARCOPHAGUS.
119. A.B. BAS-RELIEF.
120. VACANT.
121. VACANT.
122. VICTORY.

No.
123. VACANT.
124. FROM A TERRA-COTTA.
125. BAS-RELIEF.
126. BAS-RELIEF.
127. ROMAN SACRIFICE.
128. TERRA-COTTAS.
129. PUDICITIA.
129.* BAS-RELIEF.
130. CERES.
130 A. BAS-RELIEF.
131. BAS-RELIEF.
132. MUSICIANS.
133. THE MUSES.
134. BAS-RELIEF.
135. BAS-RELIEF.
136. BAS-RELIEF.
137. BAS-RELIEF.
138. ALTO-RILIEVO OF WHITE MARBLE.
139. BAS-RELIEF.
140. BAS-RELIEF.
141. THREE CITIES PERSONIFIED.
142. VESTAL.
143. BAS-RELIEF.
144. RETROGRADE SEPULCHRAL INSCRIPTION.
145. SMALL BAS-RELIEF.
146. ATHENIAN BAS-RELIEF.
147. THE DIOSCURI.
148. PORTION OF A FUNEREAL VASE.
149. CIPPUS.
150. UPPER PART OF DORIC COLUMN OF THE PARTHENON.
151. BAS-RELIEF.
152. ATHENIAN BAS-RELIEF.
153. A VERY FINE FRAGMENT.
154. ALTO-RILIEVO FROM ATHENS.
155. PLUTO.
156. FRAGMENT OF FRIEZE OF THE PARTHENON.
157. FRAGMENT OF A HORSE'S HEAD.
158. SMALL BAS-RELIEF.
159. BAS-RELIEF.
160. JUNO AND MINERVA.
161. A CAVALCADE.
162. AN INSCRIBED STÊLÊ.
163. BAS-RELIEF.
164. THE LOWER PORTION OF A STÊLÊ.
165. JUNO.
166. BAS-RELIEF.
167. A SMALL ATHENIAN BAS-RELIEF.
168. BAS-RELIEF.
169. A LOW RELIEF.
170. CARYATIDÆ.
171. BAS-RELIEF.
172. ULYSSES AND HIS DOG.
173. AN INSCRIBED FAREWELL SCENE.
174. AN INTERESTING LITTLE ALTO-RILIEVO.
175. BAS-RELIEF.
176. FRAGMENT OF SEATED FEMALE.
177. FRAGMENT.
178 and 178A. ALTO-RILIEVO.

No.
178B.
THE ELGIN MARBLES.
FRIEZE.
EAST FRIEZE.
179. A PORTION OF THE WEST FRIEZE OF THE PARTHENON.
180. FRAGMENT OF THE FRIEZE OF THE PARTHENON IN THE VATICAN.
181. PORTION OF AN INTERESTING LITTLE FEMALE FIGURE.
182. FRAGMENT OF ONE OF THE SOUTH METOPES OF THE PARTHENON.
183. VACANT.
184. VACANT.
STATUES FROM THE EASTERN PEDIMENT OF THE PARTHENON.
185. THESEUS.
185A. CERES AND PROSERPINE.
185C. HORSE'S HEAD.
186B. THE FATES.
187. NIOBÊ AND DAUGHTER.
187A. NIOBID.
187B. NIOBID.
187C. NIOBID AND PÆDAGOGUE.
187D. NIOBID.
187E. NIOBID.
187F. NIOBID.
187G. NIOBID.
187H. NIOBID.
187I. NIOBID.
187K. NIOBID.
187L. NIOBID.
188. COLOSSAL TORSO.
189. THE ILIONEUS RESTORED.
190. VENUS.
191. CUPID.
192. THE SON OF NIOBÊ.
193. FARNESE TORSO OF A YOUTH.
194. AMAZON.
195. PRIEST OF BACCHUS.
196. MELPOMENÊ.
197. ILIONEUS.
198. MEDICI VENUS.
199. PSYCHE.
200. OWL UPON A SQUARE PLINTH.
201. IRIS, HECATE, OR LUCIFERA.
202. PAN.
203. CUPID.
204. MODEL OF THE TEMPLE OF NEPTUNE AT PÆSTUM.
205. SQUARE ALTAR OF THE CAPITOL.
206. SOSIBIUS VASE.
207. FUNEREAL VASE.
208. SACRIFICIAL ALTAR.
209. CANDELABRUM OR TRIPOD.
210. ALTAR.
211. A TRIPOD.
212. VICTORY.
213. CINERARIUM OF LUCILIUS.
215. EURIPIDES.
216. CANDELABRUM.
217. HEAD OF MAGNUS DECENTIUS.

We walk through this court until we reach the nave; then turning to the left find ourselves facing the

ROMAN COURT.

On approaching this Court the visitor will at once notice a new architectural element—as useful as it is beautiful—namely, the ARCH, a feature that has been found susceptible of the greatest variety of treatment. Until within the last few years the credit of the first use of the arch as an *architectural principle* has been given to the Greek architect under Roman rule, but discoveries in Egypt, and more recently in Assyria by Mr. Layard and M. Botta, have shown that constructed and ornamented arches were frequently employed in architecture many hundred years before the Christian era. It is to be observed that architecture and sculpture had no original growth at Rome,

and were not indigenous to the soil. Roman structures were modifications from the Greek, adapted to suit the requirements and tastes of the people ; and thus it happened that the simple severity, purity, and ideality of early Greek art degenerated under the Roman empire, into the wanton luxuriousness that characterized its latest period. In comparing the Greek and Roman statues, we remark a grandeur of conception, a delicacy of sentiment, a poetical refinement of thought in the former, indicative of the highest artistic development with which we are acquainted. When Greece became merely a Roman province, that high excellence was already on the decline, and the dispersion of her artists, on the final subjugation of the country by Mummius, the Roman general, B.C. 146, hastened the descent. A large number of Grecian artists settled at Rome, where the sentiment of servitude, and the love of their masters for display, produced works which by degrees fell further and further from their glorious models, until richness of material, manual cunning, and a more than feminine weakness characterized their principal productions ; and the sculptor's art became degraded into a trade, in which all feeling for the ancient Greek excellence was for ever lost.

B 2

Thus, in the transplanted art of Greece, serving its Roman masters, a material and sensual feeling more or less prevails, appealing to the passions rather than to the intellects and high imaginations of men. The cumbrous dresses and armour which mark the properly Roman style, hide the graceful and powerful forms of nature under the symbols of station and office, creating a species of political sculpture.

Statue of Hadrian from the British Museum.

In the wall now before us we have a model of a portion of the outer wall of the Coliseum at Rome, pierced with arches and ornamented with Tuscan columns. The Coliseum is one of the most wonderful structures in the world, and the Pyramids of Egypt alone can be compared with it in point of size. It is elliptical in form, and consisted outwardly of four stories. In the centre of the interior was the *arena* or scene of action, around which the seats for spectators rose, tier above tier. The enormous range was capable of seating 87,000 persons. Vespasian and Titus erected this amphitheatre, and the work commenced about A.D. 79. In this vast and splendidly decorated building, the ancient Romans assembled to witness chariot-races, naval engagements, combats of wild animals, and other exciting sports.

Entering the Roman Court through the central archway we come into an apartment whose walls are coloured in imitation of the porphyry, malachite, and rare marbles with which the Roman people loved to adorn their houses. This style of decoration appears to have been introduced a little before the Christian era, and so lavish were the Romans in supplying ornament for their homes, that the Emperor Augustus, dreading the result of the extravagance, endeavoured by his personal moderation to put a stop to the reckless expenditure: although, it is recorded, that the lofty exemplar was set up for imitation in vain.

Following the same plan as in the Greek Court, we proceed round from the right to the left, examining the sculptures and models. Amongst the former will be noticed the statue of Drusus from Naples (222); the beautiful Venus Aphrodite from the Capitol, Rome (226); the Venus Genitrix from the Louvre (228); the fine statue of a musician, or female performer on the lyre, from the Louvre (230); the Marine Venus (233); the Venus of Arles (237); the Venus Callipygos from Naples (238); and the Bacchus from the Louvre (241).* Around the court are placed the portrait busts of the most celebrated kings and emperors of Rome, arranged chronologically, commencing, on the right hand side of the entrance, with Numa Pompilius (34), and terminating with Constantinus Chlorus (73)†. Amongst the models is one of the Coliseum, which will give the visitor a perfect idea of the form and arrangement, if not of the size, of the original structure. Having completed our survey, we enter the arched vestibule at the back adjoining the Greek Court. This vestibule, and the three others adjacent, are founded, in respect of their decorations and paintings, on examples still extant in the ancient baths of Rome. The bath, as is well known, was indispensable to the Romans, and in the days of their "decadence," when they had sunk from glorious conquerors and mighty generals into the mere indolent slaves of luxury, the warm bath was used to excess. It is said that it was resorted to as often as seven or eight times a day, and even used immediately after a meal, to assist the digestive organs, and to enable the bather to enjoy, with as little delay as possible, another luxurious repast.

We proceed through these vestibules, as in the Greek Court, studying the objects of art, and occasionally stepping out to notice the continuation of the Parthenon frieze on the wall at the back, and the sculptures ranged around. In the centre of the first vestibule is the Venus Genitrix (234); in the centre of the second vestibule, the Apollo Belvedere (252); and in the third, the Diana with the deer (261)‡,—three chef-d'œuvres of sculpture, that give an idea of the highest state of art under Roman rule. We soon arrive at the sides of the Alhambra, when, turning to the right, we find ourselves in a Roman side court, which is surrounded by the busts of the most renowned Roman Generals, of Empresses and other women.

* These numbers refer to the Handbook of the Roman Court.
† These two numbers refer to those in the Handbook to the Portrait Gallery.
‡ Numbers of Roman Handbook.

ANTIQUE SCULPTURES IN ROMAN COURT AND NAVE.

No.

218. MODEL OF THE FORUM OF ROME.
221. FAUN.
222. STATUE OF DRUSUS.
223. YOUNG FAUN.
224. DRAPED VENUS AND CUPID.
225. YOUNG HERCULES.
226. VENUS OF THE CAPITOL.
227. GANYMEDES.
228. VENUS GENITRIX.
229. GIRL.
230. PORTRAIT OF A MUSICIAN.
231. SMALL FEMALE FIGURE.
232. YOUTH INVOKING THE GODS.
233. MARINE VENUS AND CUPID.
234. CAMILLUS.
235. LARGE FEMALE FIGURE.
236. VENUS.
237. VENUS VICTRIX.
238. VENUS CALLIPYGOS.
239. URANIA.
240. BACCHUS.
241. RICHELIEU BACCHUS.
242. FAUN.
243. VENUS AND CUPID.
244. FEMALE READING A SCROLL.
245. VENUS.
246. CUPID AND PSYCHE.
247. BOY EXTRACTING THORN.
248. VENUS.
249. CERES.
250. ANCHIRRHÖE.
251. NYMPH EXTRACTING A THORN.
252. BELVEDERE APOLLO.
253. YOUNG FAUN.
254. CUPID.
255. HERCULES AND OMPHALE.
256. YOUNG FAUN.
257. FAUN.
258. APOLLO SAUROCTONOS.
259. FAUN.
260. YOUNG FAUN.
261. DIANA.
262. BOY AND GOOSE.
263. BOY AND BIRD.
264. BOY WITH MASK.
265. URANIA.
266. PENELOPE.
267. GANYMEDES.
268. GIRL.
269. BOY AND GOOSE.
270. EUMACHIA.
271. PUDICITIA.
272. PORTRAIT STATUE OF A ROMAN LADY.
273. LIVIA DRUSILLA.
274. VASE.
275. CANDELABRUM.
276. TORLONIA HERCULES.
277. DOG.
278. COLOSSAL CUPID AS HERCULES.
279. BACCHUS.
280. ANTINOUS.
281. AGRIPPINA THE ELDER.
282. ADONIS.
283. BACCHUS.

No.

284. FAUN OF THE CAPITOL.
285. MERCURY.
286. TRAJAN.
287. MERCURY OF THE VATICAN.
288. ANTINOUS.
289. MELEAGER OF BERLIN.
290. MENANDER.
291. POSIDIPPUS.
292. BOAR.
293. MELEAGER OF THE VATICAN.
294. QUOIT-PLAYER.
295. FAUN.
296. ADONIS.
297. POLYHYMNIA.
298. APOLLO SAUROCTONOS.
299. ATHLETE, OR BOXER.
300. THE CLAPPING FAUN.
301. APOLLO SAUROCTONOS.
302. AMAZON.
303. FAUN.
304. WRESTLERS.
305. YOUNG FAUN.
306. SILENUS.
307. POSIDONIUS.
308. DEMOSTHENES.
309. GLADIATOR.
310. ACHILLES.
311. BACCHUS.
312. GERMANICUS.
313. ADONIS, OR APOLLO.
314. ANTINOUS.
315. DISCOBOLUS.
316. MERCURY.
317. HERCULES.
318 and 319. DIOSCURI.
319. VACANT.
320. MONUMENT OF LYSICRATES.
321. DEMOSTHENES.
322. SOPHOCLES.
323. VACANT.
324. PHOCION.
325. VACANT.
326. ARISTIDES, OR ÆSCHINES.
327. PHILOSOPHER.
328. MINERVA.
329. MELPOMENE.
330. YOUNG JUPITER.
331. LUCIUS VERUS.
332. PLOTINA.
333. LUCIUS VERUS.
334. JULIA PIA DOMNA.
335. JUNO.
336. MEDUSA HEAD.
337. OLYMPIAN JUPITER.
338. TITUS VESPASIAN.
339. JUPITER SERAPIS.
340. MARINE DEITY.
341. JUNO.
342. PERTINAX.
343. TRAJAN.
344. MARCUS AURELIUS.
345. M. AGRIPPA.
346. THALIA.
347. ANTINOUS.
348. HEAD OF THE YOUTHFUL BACCHUS.

No.
349. JUNO.
350. DIRCE.
351. PALLAS.
352. BORGHESE VASE.
353. MEDICI VASE.
354. VASE.
355. VASE.
356. VASE.
357. FOUNTAIN IN FORM OF A TRIPOD.
358. CUPID ENCIRCLED BY A DOLPHIN.
359. AMAZON.
360. CERES.
361. MERCURY.
362. MEDICI VENUS.
363. ATHLETE.
364. POSIDONIUS.
365. POLYHYMNIA.
366. BRONZE STATUE OF A YOUTH.
367. FAUN.
368. ANTINOUS AND HIS GENIUS.
369. DANCING FAUN.
370. SLEEPING FAUN.
371. BUST OF MELEAGER.
372. BRONZE FAUN.
373. APOLLO SAUROCTONOS.
374. SMALL SITTING FIGURE OF URANIA.
375. BRONZE STATUE OF A YOUTH.
376. SMALL FIGURE OF CERES.
377. APOLLO LYCIUS.
378. THE DOG MOLOSSUS.
379. WRESTLERS, OR PANCRATIASTÆ.
380. BRONZE STATUE OF A BOY EX-
     TRACTING A THORN.
381. ANTONINUS PIUS.
382. INDIAN BACCHUS.
383. BUST OF LAUGHING FAUN.
384. BUST OF ACHILLES.
385. DOUBLE HERMES, OR TERMINAL BUST.
386. BEARDED BACCHUS.
387. BACCHUS.
388. ZEUS TROPHONIOS.
389. HEAD OF APOLLO.
390. JUPITER.
391. DOUBLE HERMES, OR TERMINAL BUST.
392. HEAD OF APOLLO.
393. JUPITER SERAPIS.
394. THE SUN.
395. JUNO.
396. APOLLO.
397. HEAD OF THE LAOCOON.
398. ACHILLES.
399. ÆSCULAPIUS.
400. FEMALE BUST.
401. PHILOSOPHER.
402. BUST OF DRAPED FEMALE.
403. PLUTO.
404. OMPHALE.
405. BUST OF ARIADNE, OR ARETHUSA.
406. SERAPIS, OR INFERNAL JUPITER.
407. PARIS.
408. BUST OF MINERVA MEDICA.
409. BUST OF PALLAS.
410. MEDUSA.
411. BUST OF REPOSING FAUN.
412. HEAD OF A CHILD.
413. JUPITER.

No.
414. PART OF A SEPULCHRAL ALTAR.
415. OMPHALE.
416. STAG REARING.
417. ROEBUCK STANDING.
418. NYMPH.
419. NYMPH AT FOUNTAIN.
420. SMALL STATUE OF SITTING HER-
     CULES.
421. CATO AND PORCIA.
422. BRONZE PLATES FROM ETRUSCAN
     CHARIOT.
423. ÆSOP STATUE.
     Not yet arrived.
219. MODEL OF THE COLISEUM AT ROME.
220. MODEL OF THE TRAJAN COLUMN AT
     ROME.
ADORANTE.
ADORANTE.
ÆNEAS.
ÆSCULAPIUS.
ARIADNE.
BAS-RELIEF OF A COMIC SCENE.
BAS-RELIEF.
BOY AND GOOSE.
BUST OF SCIPIO AFRICANUS.
CENTAUR BORGHESE.
CERES.
CROUCHING VENUS.
DOMITIAN.
EUTERPE.
FLORA.
FLORENCE HERMAPHRODITE.
HERCULES.
HERMAPHRODITE.
HERMAPHRODITE.
INDIAN BACCHUS.
INDIAN BACCHUS.
INDIAN BACCHUS.
ISIS.
ISIS.
JUNO.
JUNO OF THE CAPITOL.
JUPITER SERAPIS.
LA PROVIDENCE.
MENELAUS BUST.
MINERVA BUST.
MUSE.
NEBRID BACCHUS.
NIOBE SARCOPHAGUS.
PÆTUS AND ARRIA.
PALÆMON.
PROVIDENTIA.
ROME.
ROME.
SALPION VASE.
SIBYL.
THE TRIUMPH OF TITUS.
THE MOST CELEBRATED BERNINI HER-
MAPHRODITE.
TIBERIUS.
TRIANGULAR ALTAR OF THE TWELVE
GODS.
VASE OF THE CAPITOL.
VENUS OF CNIDOS.
WOUNDED AMAZON.
YOUNG HERCULES.

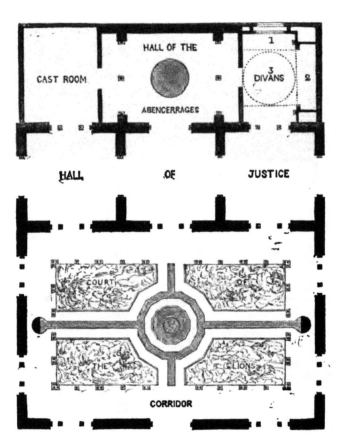

GROUND PLAN OF THE ALHAMBRA.

Passing through this compartment, we once more make our way to the nave, and bring ourselves face to face with the gorgeous magnificence of

Outer Walls of the Alhambra.

THE ALHAMBRA COURT.

The architectural sequence is now interrupted. We have arrived at one of those offshoots from a parent stem which flourished for a time, and then entirely disappeared : leaving examples of their art which either compel our wonder by the extraordinary novelty of the details, as in the case of Nineveh, or, as in the court now before us, excite our admiration to the highest pitch, by the splendour and richness of the decorations. The Saracenic or Moresque architecture sprang from the Byzantine, the common parent of all subsequent styles, and the legitimate successor to the Roman system. We shall immediately have occasion to speak more particularly of the parent root when we cross the nave and enter the Byzantine Court. Of the Moorish architecture which branched out from it, it will be sufficient to say here that the solid external structure was of plain, simple masonry ; whilst the inside was literally covered, from end to end, with rich arabesque work in coloured stucco, and adorned with mosaic pavements, marble fountains, and sweet-smelling flowers.

The fortress-palace of the Alkambra,* of a portion of which this court is a reproduction, was built about the middle of the thirteenth century. It rises on a hill above the city of Granada (in the south of Spain), the capital of the Moorish kingdom of that name, which, for two hundred and fifty years, withstood the repeated attacks of the Christians, and was not finally reduced until 1492, by Ferdinand and Isabella. The Alhambra, under Moorish rule, was the scene of the luxurious pleasures of the monarch, and the stage upon which many fearful crimes were enacted. Within its brilliant courts, the king fell by the hand of the aspiring chief, who, in his turn, was cut down by an equally ambitious rival. Few spots can boast a more intimate association with the romantic than the Alhambra, until the Christians ejected the Moors from their splendid home, and the palace of the unbeliever became a Christian fortress.

The part here reproduced is the far-famed Court of Lions and the Tribunal of Justice. The outside of these courts is covered with diaper work, consisting of inscriptions in Arabic character, of conventional representation of flowers and of flowing decoration, over which the eye wanders, delighted with the harmony of the colouring and the variety of the ornament. Entering through the central archway, we see before us the fountain supported by the lions that give name to the court ; and, through the archway opposite, a portion of the stalactite roof of the Hall of the Abencerrages. Around and about us on every side highly ornamental surfaces attract and ravish the vision. We gaze on the delicate fretwork of the arches, on the exquisite pattern of the gorgeous illumination, we listen to the pleasant music of falling waters, and inhale the fragrant perfume of flowers, until, carried away by the force of imagination we live in an age of chivalry, and amidst the influences of oriental life. This court is 75 feet long, just two-thirds the length of the original ; the columns are as high as the

---

* (The Red) probably so called either from the colour of the soil, or from the deep red brick of which it is built.

columns of the Court of Lions itself, and the arches that spring from them are also of the actual size of the original arches. Over the columns is inscribed in Cufic characters "*And there is no Conqueror but God.*" Round the basin of the fountain is an Arabic poem, from which we take two specimens :—

> " Oh thou who beholdest these Lions crouching—fear not !
> Life is wanting to enable them to show their fury ! "

Less, we must think, a needless caution to the intruder, than the poet's allowed flattery to his brother artist. In the verse of

Stucco Ornament from the Alhambra.

Greece and modern Italy, we find the same heightened expression of admiration for the almost animating art of sculpture. The following passage is oriental in every letter :—

> " Seest thou not how the water flows on the surface,
> notwithstanding the current strives to oppose its progress.
> Like a lover whose eyelids are pregnant with tears, and
> who suppresses them for fear of a tale-bearer."

Through this brilliant court, the visitor will proceed or linger as his fascinated spirit directs. There are no statues to examine, for the religion of the Moors forbade the representation of living objects; in truth, the exquisitely wrought tracery on every

Arabesque ornament from the Alhambra.

side upon which the Moorish mind was thus forced to concentrate all its artistic power and skill, is in itself sufficient exclusively to arrest and to enchain the attention. A curious infringement, however, of the Mahommedan law just now mentioned, which proscribes the representation of natural objects, is observable in the lions supporting the fountain, and in three paintings, which occupy a portion of the original ceilings in the Tribunal of Justice and the two alcoves adjoining. It is also to be remarked that, although the followers of Mahommed scrupulously avoid stepping upon a piece of paper lest the name of God should be written thereon, yet that name is found repeatedly upon the tile floor of the same tribunal. From these circumstances it would seem that the Mahommedans of the West were more lax in their observances than their brethren of the East, having in all probability imbibed some of the ideas and feelings of the Spanish Christians with whom they came in contact.

Passing through the archway opposite to that at which we entered, we find ourselves in a vestibule which in the Alhambra

Moorish bas-relief, from a Fountain at Granada.

itself leads from the Court of Lions to the Tribunal of Justice. This is, however, only a portion of the original passage. The arches opening from the central to the right and left divisions of the vestibule are of the size of the originals, the patterns on the walls and ceilings being taken from other portions of the Alhambra.

The visitor may now proceed through the left-hand arch into the division next the Roman Court. On the right of this division he will find a small room devoted to models, and specimens of the original casts of ornaments of the Alhambra, brought by Mr. Owen Jones from Spain, from which this court has been constructed. Returning to the central division, he sees on his left the Hall of the Abencerrages, already spoken of, and which, with its beautiful stalactite roof, is now in rapid course of completion. Proceeding onward, we quit the Alhambra, and emerge into the north transept.

The visitor now crosses the transept, immediately in front of the colossal sitting figures, which he will be able to examine with effect when he commences a tour through the nave, which we propose that he shall shortly make. Passing these figures then for the moment, he directs his attention to

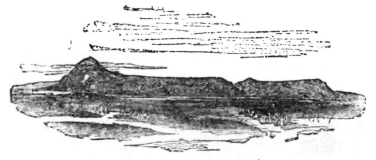

The great mound of Nimroud.

THE ASSYRIAN COURT,

which faces him.   This Court is larger than any other appropriated to the illustration of one phase of art.   It is 120 feet long, 50 feet wide, and has an elevation of 40 feet from the floor line.   Its chief interest, however, consists in the fact of its illustrating a style of art of which no specimen has hitherto been presented in Europe, and which, indeed, until the last few years, lay unknown even in the country where its remains have been unexpectedly brought to light.   It is only ten years ago that M. Botta, the French Consul at Mossul, first discovered the existence of sculptural remains of the old Assyrian empire at Khorsabad : and since that time the palace, now known to have been erected about the year 720 B.C. by Sargon, the successor of Shalmaneser, has been mainly explored, as well as the palace of his son Sennacherib at Koyunjik, and that of Esarhaddon at Nimroud, besides other older palaces in the last-named locality.   In addition to the explorations that have been made on these sites, extensive excavations and examinations also within the last few years have been made into the ruins of the palaces of Nebuchadnezzar at Babylon, and of Darius and Xerxes at Susa.

It is from the immense mass of new materials, so suddenly revealed, that Mr. James Fergusson, assisted by Mr. Layard, has erected the court before which the visitor now stands — an architectural illustration which, without pretending to be a literal copy of any one building, most certainly represents generally the architecture of the extinct but once mighty kingdoms of Mesopotamia, during the two centuries that elapsed between the reign of

Sennacherib and that of Xerxes, viz., from about B.C. 700 to B.C. 500.

The oldest form of architecture in these Eastern parts was probably that which existed in Babylon : but the absence of stone in that country reduced the inhabitants to the necessity of using bricks only, and for the most part bricks burnt by the sun, though sometimes fire-burnt brickwork is also found. The face of the walls so constructed was ornamented with paintings, either on plaster or enamelled on the bricks, whilst the constructive portions and roofs were of wood. All this perishable material has of course disappeared, and nothing now remains even of the Babylon built by Nebuchadnezzar but formless mounds of brickwork. In the more northern kingdom of Assyria, the existence of stone and marble secured a wainscoating of sculptured slabs for the palace walls, whilst great winged bulls and giant figures also in stone adorned the portals and façades. The pillars, however, which supported the roofs, and the roofs themselves, were all of wood, generally of cedar, and these having been destroyed by fire or by the lapse of ages, nothing remains to tell of their actual size and form. Yet we are not left entirely to conjecture in respect of them. Susa and Persepolis in Persia — the followers and imitators of Nineveh — arose in districts where stone was abundant, and we find that the structures in these cities had not only stone pillars to support the roof, but also stone jambs in the doorways, thus affording an unmistakeable clue to the nature of such portions of building as are wanting to complete our knowledge of the architecture of the Assyrian people.

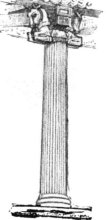

Pillar from the arcade of the Court.

As now laid bare to us, the Assyrian style of architecture differs essentially from any other with which we have hitherto been made acquainted. Its main characteristics are enormously thick mud-brick walls, covered with painted bas-reliefs, and roofs supported internally by slight but elegant wooden columns, ornamented with volutes (spiral mouldings), and the elegant honey-suckle ornament which was afterwards introduced through Ionia into Greece—this Assyrian style being, according to some, the parent of the Ionic order, as the Egyptian was of the Doric order, of Greece. As far as we can judge from descriptions, the architecture of Jerusalem was almost identical with that of Assyria.

The whole of the lower portion of the exterior front and sides of this Court is taken from the palace at Khorsabad, the great winged

Entrance to the Nineveh Court.

bulls, the giants strangling the lions, and the other features being casts from the objects sent from the site of the palace, to the Louvre, and arranged, as far as circumstances admit, in the relative position of the original objects as they were discovered. The dwarf columns on the walls with the double bull capitals, are modelled from details found at Persepolis and Susa, whilst the cornice and battlements above have been copied from representations found in one of the bas-reliefs at Khorsabad. The painting of the cornice is in strict accordance with the recent discoveries at that place.

Entering through the opening in the side, guarded by colossal bulls, the visitor finds himself in a large hall, in the centre of which stand four great columns copied literally from columns found at Susa and Persepolis. The walls of the hall are covered with sculpture, cast from originals brought to this country by Mr Layard from his excavations at Nimroud, and deposited in the British Museum. Upon the sculptures are engraved the arrow-headed inscriptions which have been so recently, and in so remarkable a manner, deciphered by Colonel Rawlinson and Dr. Hincks. Above these is a painting of animals and trees, copied from one found at Khorsabad. The roof crowning the hall represents the form of ceiling usual in that part of Asia,  but is rather a vehicle for the display of the various coloured patterns of Assyrian art than a direct copy of anything found in the Assyrian palaces. In the centre of the great hall the visitor will notice a decorated archway leading to the refreshment room. The very recent discovery of this highly ornamented arch at Khorsabad proves—somewhat unexpectedly—that the Assyrian people were far from ignorant of the value of this beautiful feature of architecture. On either side of the main entrance to this Court (from the Nave), are two small apartments, lined also with casts from sculptures at Nimroud, arranged, as nearly as may be, according to their original positions. Above them are paintings of a procession, such as occupied a similar place in the palaces of Assyria. A complete detailed account of this interesting department will be found in Mr. Layard's valuable Handbook to the Nineveh Court.

Having completed his survey of the interior of this Court, the visitor may either enter the refreshment room at the back through the archway, and then make his way to the Nave, or he may at once quit the Court by the central entrance, and turning to the left cross the north end of the Nave, stopping for one moment under the shade of the finest palm-tree in Europe, on his passage to look from end to end of the magnificent structure within which he stands, and to glance at the exterior of the Court he has just quitted, the bright colouring of which — the bold ornaments, the gigantic bulls, and colossal features, present as novel and striking an architectural and decorative display as the mind can imagine.

Having crossed the building under the gallery, the visitor will find on his left the north wing : the site appropriated for the extensive collection of Raw Produce, now forming under the hands of Professor Wilson.

RAW PRODUCE AND AGRICULTURAL COLLECTION.

This collection is intended to show, by means of a series of industrial specimens, the natural resources of this and other countries ; to teach, through the medium of the eye, the history of the various substances which the earth produces for the use of man ; to point out whence and by what means they are obtained, and how they are made subservient to our wants and comforts. The collection has thus a twofold object : First, to display what is termed the raw produce of the world, comprising substances belonging to each of the three kingdoms of nature ; and secondly, to exhibit the same produce, when converted by industry into the form of a highly-finished manufacture.

The collection consists of the three following principal divisions :

1. The Soil.
2. The Produce of the Soil.
3. The Economic and Technical Uses to which the Produce is applied.

The first grand division, " The Soil," includes specimens of all those geological formations comprising what is termed the crust of the earth. From the debris of these rocks is formed what we generally understand by the term *soil ;* but soils, as we are accustomed to see them, are considerably altered by the presence of vegetable matter, the result of the decomposition of plants, and of artificial substances applied as manure. Accordingly, specimens of the *natural* sorts of various geological formations (or, in fact, the rocks merely in their disintegrated form), together with the same soils altered by cultivation, and samples of the manures which assist in changing their qualities, form an important series in this division. Besides giving rise to the different agricultural soils, the rocks of most formations are interesting as producing objects of economic value. From many such rocks are obtained building stone, slates, tiles, clays used in brick-making, flints used in glass, alum, salt, and other useful articles. These, in the present collection, are illustrated by specimens ; and when any of such substances give rise to a branch of industry, a complete illustrative series is presented to the contemplation of the visitor.

For example : it will be found that in the case of ceramic ware or pottery, the series commences with flint, which is shown first in its natural state as it comes from the chalk pits, then calcined and ground, and then re-calcined. Next we see it mixed with clay, afterwards moulded into the form of a vase, and lastly baked. To these different specimens, it will be noted, are added samples of the colour used in the ornamentation of the object.

By far the most important and useful mineral product is coal, of which specimens of different qualities, suited to various purposes, are exhibited from foreign countries, as well as from all the coal fields of Great Britain.

From the rocks of different formations we obtain the ores of metals, the principal of which in this country are iron, lead, copper, and tin. Other metals are found, but in smaller quantities than elsewhere. Metals are not generally found *native*, but in the form of oxides, sulphides, &c., and must therefore undergo considerable changes before they can be made available. The methods of extracting metals from their ores, as practised in this and other countries, and the various uses to which the metals are applied, are amply illustrated by specimens from all the principal works, and form, perhaps, the most instructive and important feature of the mineral division of the Raw Produce collection.

The second great division, "The Produce of the Soil," resolves itself naturally into two principal groups : viz., vegetable substances, or the *direct* produce of the soil, and animal substances, the *secondary* produce of the soil. The chief sub-divisions of these groups are :

a. Substances used as food, such as tea, coffee, fruits (amongst vegetable substances), and meats, gelatine, lard, &c. (amongst animal products).

b. Substances used in the arts, manufactures, &c., as flax, hemp, cork, gums, dye-stuffs (in the vegetable kingdom), and wools, silk, horns, skins, oils, &c. (in the animal kingdom).

And these are again classed as Home and Foreign products.

The third great division, "The Economic or Technical Uses to which the Produce is applied," is a most important feature of this department. The want of a "Trades' Museum" in England has long been felt by commercial and scientific men, and until now no attempt at any collection of the kind has been made. The technological illustrations about to be here produced in a great measure supply the desideratum, and present, so to speak, a series of *eye lectures* that carry with them an amount of information no less instructive than important to the progressive industry of the kingdom.

In this division each series is commenced by examples of the raw material, which is carried by illustrative specimens through the various processes to which it is submitted before it reaches its highest value as a manufactured article.   The visitor also finds in this series models, &c., of the machinery used in the manufactures. As an example of the instruction afforded in this division, we will take the manufacture of linen.   The first sample seen is the flax plant.   This produces linseed and flax straw.   The former is pressed, and we have linseed oil and oil cake.   The straw is steeped, broken, and scutched, and we have rough fibre.   The rough fibre is *heckled*, and is then ready for spinning.   The refuse which is heckled out is tow.   The heckled fibre is spun into yarns of different degrees of fineness, which are woven into linen of various qualities.   Finally, the linen is *bleached*.   The tow is used for paper-making, for string and cordage, or is spun into coarse thread, called tow-line, and woven into rough fabrics.   The technical application of animal substances is treated in a similar manner.

The third division, as in the case of the second, is sub-divided into articles used as food, and those used in the arts, &c., and is also similarly separated into smaller groups of home and foreign produce ; and again, as far as the plan admits of carrying out, into manufactures dependent upon chemical, and manufactures dependent upon mechanical agencies.

Leaving the north wing, and returning up the aisle, on the garden side of the Palace, we come, following the order of the architectural arrangement, upon the

THE BYZANTINE AND ROMANESQUE COURT.

Before the visitor is conducted through the architectural Courts on this side of the Nave, it is necessary he should understand that they differ considerably in arrangement and treatment from those on the opposite side, which have already been described.   In the Egyptian, Greek, and other Courts through which he has passed, the forms or characteristics of some one distinctive structure have, to a greater or less extent, been given ; but the Courts into which we are now about to penetrate, are not architectural restorations, but rather so many collections of ornamental details stamped with unmistakeable individuality, and enabling us at a glance to recognise and distinguish the several styles that have existed and succeeded each other, from the beginning of the 6th down to the

Byzantine Court (entrance from North Transept).

16th century. In each Court will be found important details, ornament, and even entire portions, taken from the most remarkable or beautiful edifices of the periods they illustrate. Thus the palaces and Christian temples of Italy, the castles and churches of Germany, the hotels-de-ville and chateaux of Belgium and France, and the cathedrals and mansions in our own country, have all been laid under contribution, so that here, for the first time in the history of architecture, we have the opportunity of acquiring a perceptive and practical knowledge of the beautiful art during the period of its later progress.

The regular architectural sequence on the other side of the Nave finds its termination in the Roman Court, and we now resume the order of history with the "Byzantine" Court. Art, as we have already indicated, declined during the Roman Empire; but the general adoption of Christianity gave the blow that finally overthrew it, for the introduction of this faith was, unfortunately, accompanied with bitter and violent enmity against all pagan forms of beauty. An edict of Theodosius, in the early part of the 5th century, ordered that pagan art should be utterly annihilated, and the primitive Christians demolished with fanatic zeal the temples, bronzes, paintings, and statues that adorned the Roman capital.

To complete the work of destruction, it is related that Gregory (A.D. 590) one of the celebrated "Fathers" of the Roman Church, gave orders that every vestige of Pagan Rome should be consigned to the Tiber; and thus was ancient Art smitten and overthrown, and the attempt made to efface its very foot-prints from the earth; so that, indeed, men had now to proceed as best they might, by painful and laborious efforts, towards the formation of a new and essentially Christian style of architecture, which, however feeble and badly imitated from ancient models at its commencement, was finally productive of the most original and beautiful results.

Constantine the Great, in the early part of the 4th century, embraced Christianity. The new religion required structures capable of holding large assemblages of people at certain periods; and notwithstanding the magnificence of some of the Roman structures, none could be found appropriate to the required use, save the Basilicas, or Halls of Justice, at Rome. The form of these structures was oblong, and the interior consisted of a central avenue and two side aisles, divided from the centre by a double row of columns, the central avenue terminating in a semicircular recess with the roof rounded off. It will be at once apparent that such buildings were admirably adapted to the purposes and observances of the new religion; and, accordingly, in A.D. 323, when Constantine removed the seat of empire from the West to the East, from Rome to Byzantium (Constantinople), the Roman Basilica probably served as a model for the Christian churches which he rapidly raised in his new city.

But on this point we have little authentic information; time, the convulsions of nature, and the destructive hand of man, have long since lost to us the original churches built on Constantine's settlement at Byzantium, and the oldest monument with which we are acquainted, that of Santa Sophia, built in the early part of the 6th century by Justinian, bears no relation in its plan to the long basilica of the Western Empire.

The great characteristic of Byzantine church architecture was a plan formed on the Greek cross; and surmounted at its points of intersection by a central dome. The direct imitation of the

Greek Cross.   Latin Cross.

antique capitals was eschewed, and a foliated capital was introduced in its place, varying considerably in pattern even in the same building : the arch was in general semicircular, and the use of mosaic ornament universal, but it was some time before the Byzantine style received its full development ; for the earlier Christians generally maintained a profound antipathy to all Art, as ostentatious, and savouring over-much of worldly delights. It is not, however, in the nature of man to exist for any length of time in this world, wondrously adorned as it is by its Divine Creator, without imbibing a love for the adornment so profusely displayed around him. This natural feeling, which St. Augustine and the stricter Christians vainly sought to decry and repress, was strengthened and aided by the more forcible notion of holding out some attraction to the pagans, who, accustomed to the ceremonies and charms of their old rites, might be repelled by the apparent gloominess of the new creed. As the number of converts increased, a demand for church ornament made itself felt, and Art once more awoke, not in the excelling beauty of its former life, but rude, unpolished, and crippled by religious necessity, which placed, as in Egypt of old, a restriction upon the forms of nature, lest by copying them the people should relapse into the idolatrous worship of graven images. In the Eastern or Greek Church, even the rude and grotesque sculpture first allowed was speedily forbidden and banished for ever. The mosaic painting, however, was continued by Greek artists, and this peculiar style of ornamentation is one of the most distinctive features of Byzantine architecture. Not only were the walls and ceilings covered with extraordinarily rich examples of glass mosaic work, formed into pictures illustrative of Scripture subjects and saintly legends, or arranged in elaborate patterns of geometrical and other ornament, but columns, pulpits, &c., were rendered brilliant with

its glowing colours. Mosaic work also is at times found on the
façades of the Byzantine buildings; whilst the pavement, if less
gorgeous, was at least as richly ornamented with coloured inlay of
Marble mosaic. As we have, however, just observed, the fear of
idolatry led to the comparative neglect of sculpture, and the edict
forbidding the sculpture of images for religious purposes became
one cause of the separation of the Latin Church in Rome from
the Greek Church in Constantinople, and thenceforth the two
churches remain distinct. In the former, sculpture continued to
exist, not as an independent art, but as a mere architectural
accessory.

Byzantine architecture flourished from A.D. 328 to 1453: but
the Byzantine proper can be said to extend only from the 6th to
the 11th centuries. Romanesque
architecture in its various deve-
lopments was more or less im-
pressed with the Byzantine character, and in its general features
resembles the source from which
it was in a great measure derived;
although the dome is generally
absent in the churches of northern
Europe, which retained the plan
of the old Roman basilica in
preference to that of the Greek
cross, for a long time peculiar to
the Eastern Church.

Romanesque Tower.

It would not be hazarding
too much, to assert that Byzantine architecture was generally adopted throughout most
European countries from the 6th
to the 11th century, with such
modifications as the necessities
of climate, the differences of
creed, and the means of building
necessitated.

Before entering this Court the visitor will do well to examine
its external decoration, affording, as it does, not only an excellent
notion of the splendid mosaic ornament we have already alluded
to as peculiarly Byzantine, but for its paintings of illustrious
characters of the Byzantine period, taken from valuable illumina-

tions and mosaics still in existence ; such as, the fine portraits of
Justinian and his consort Theodora, from Ravenna (by the entrance
from the Nave), and those of Charles the Bald of France, and the
Emperor Nicephorus Botoniates of Constantinople, copied from
valuable existing authorities ; whilst an allegorical representation
of Night, on the return side, is a proof that the poetry of Art
was not altogether dead in the 10th century, to which date it
belongs.

Byzantine Court—Arches from the Nave.

In front of all the Courts facing the Nave, are placed many very
interesting examples of Mediæval and Renaissance Art, a brief
notice of which will be found later in this volume, under the head
of " A Tour through the Nave."

The entrance to the gallery at the back of the Byzantine Court
is formed by the Chancel Arch of Tuam Cathedral in Ireland,
built about the beginning or middle of the 13th century, a most
interesting relic of art in the Sister Isle.

Entering through the arches at the North end, we turn to the
right into a cool cloister of the Romanesque school, a restored

copy of a cloister at the church of Santa Maria in Capitolo at Cologne, an ancient edifice said to have been commenced about the year 700. The cloister is, however, of the close of the 10th century. The restoration gives us an excellent notion of the arches, columns, and capitals of this period, and shows the difference that exists between Byzantine and ancient Greek or Roman art. Proceeding through the cloister, the roof of which is beautifully decorated with Byzantine ornament, in imitation of the glass mosaic work, we remark various pieces of sculpture, chiefly from Venice: at the extreme end, to the left on entering, is a recumbent effigy of Richard Cœur de Lion, from Rouen; at the farthest end, to the right, is placed the Prior's doorway from Ely, in a late Norman style, and next to this, to the right, a representation of the Baptism of Christ, from St. Mark's, at Venice. Returning to the central entrance from the Nave, we enter the Court itself. The black marble fountain in the centre is an exact copy of one at Heisterbach on the Rhine. We may now obtain some notion of the different features which mark the Byzantine, the German Romanesque, and Norman styles, all agreeing in general character, but all varying in treatment. The cloister we have just quitted, with the cubical capitals of its external columns and its profuse mosaics, presents a strongly marked impress of the Byzantine style, the same influence being also remarked in the external mosaic-work of the small but beautiful portion of the cloisters of St. John Lateran at Rome; on each side of which are fine examples of German Romanesque, which is frequently also called the Lombard style, as indicative of its origin; and beyond these again, in the extreme angles, are interesting specimens of the Norman style as practised in England during the twelfth century. These examples will enable the visitor to judge in some measure of the differences that characterize the three. To the left is a very curious Norman doorway, from Kilpeck Church, in Herefordshire; the zigzag moulding around it is peculiar to the Norman; and in the sculptured reliefs

Arch and column from Cloister.

which surround the doorway a symbolism is hidden, for the meaning of which we must refer our readers to the Handbook of this Court. Next to this is a doorway from Mayence Cathedral, the bronze doors within it, which are from Augsburgh Cathedral, in Germany, being interesting examples of the art of bronze-casting in the latter half of the 11th century. The rudely-executed subjects in the panels are mostly taken from the Old Testament, but no attempt at chronological arrangement has been made. Above the St. John Lateran cloister is an arcade from Gelnhausen in Germany, a good specimen of grotesque and symbolic sculpture quite in the style of the early Lombard work in northern Italy. The doorway on the opposite side of the St. John Lateran cloister is a composition showing the general characteristics of the Romanesque style; the doors are from Hildesheim Cathedral, and were executed in 1015, by order of Bishop Bernwardus. They contain sixteen panels, arranged in proper order, eight representing scenes in the Old Testament, commencing with the creation of man, and eight representing subjects from the New Testament, beginning with the Annunciation. Next to this, and corresponding to the Kilpeck doorway, is a second side door from Shobdon Church, Herefordshire. The circles ornamented with foliage over the Shobdon Chancel Arch, are from Moissac. On the side wall next to the Arch, is the monument, from Salisbury Cathedral, of Bishop Roger, who died A.D. 1139; it is transitional in style, from the Norman to the Early English.

On either side of the fountain in this Court, are placed the celebrated effigies of Fontevrault Abbey, (the burying-place of the Plantagenets), consisting of Henry II. and his Queen Eleonora; Richard I.; and Isabella, wife of King John. These date from the 13th century, and they are not only interesting as works of art, but valuable as portraits, and as evidences of costumes of that period. An effigy of King John from Worcester, and another of Berengaria, wife of Richard I., from the Abbey of L'Espan, near Mans in France, are also to be found here.

The inlaid marble pavement of the Court is copied from churches in Florence, and is of the beginning of the 13th century.

Having thoroughly examined the various contents of this Court, we pass through the opening in the arcade of St. John Lateran, before mentioned, and enter a vestibule, the vaulting of which is from the convent of the Franciscans, at Assisi, in Central Italy, with the paintings in the four compartments of the vault, from their originals by Cimabue.

In the centre of this compartment is a large black marble Norman font from Winchester Cathedral : the date of which has given rise to much controversy ; those assigned, ranging from 630 to 1150. Next to this font is another from Eardsley Church, Herefordshire, of the 12th century.

Passing now to the left, we see on the back wall, looking towards the Garden, three openings, the central one of which is a doorway from the church of Freshford, in Kilkenny, of about the latter end of the 11th or beginning of the 12th century, and on either side of it, are windows from the church of Tuam, in Ireland. Above the Freshford doorway is a large circular window from Rathain Church, remarkable for its great antiquity, and said to have been erected as early as the middle of the 8th century. In this compartment are also placed Irish crosses, affording examples of the sculptural antiquities of the Sister Isle ; and some interesting crosses from the Isle of Man. Having examined this compartment, we proceed for a short distance southwards, down the corridor or gallery, and pass, on the back wall of the Byzantine Court, first, a doorway composed principally from an existing example at Romsey Abbey, the bas-relief in the door-head being from Shobdon : and on the other side of the St. John Lateran arcade, a beautiful Norman doorway from Birkin Church, Yorkshire : after which we reach the smaller division of the Mediæval Court, dedicated to works of German Mediæval Art, the entrance to which is beneath the Pointed arcade on our right.

Door from Birkin Church.

THE GERMAN MEDIÆVAL COURT.

This small Court is devoted exclusively to examples of Gothic art and architecture in Germany, and, taken with the English and French Mediæval Courts,—which we shall presently reach,—gives an excellent idea of the style and character of architecture in these three countries during the Middle Ages. Such remarks as are required to explain the transition from the Romanesque and Byzantine to the Pointed style of architecture, we shall defer until we find ourselves in the Mediæval Court of our own country. We, therefore, without preface, conduct the visitor from the gallery of the Byzantine Court, through the side arches directly into the German Mediæval Court. The large doorway in the centre at once attracts attention. This is cast from a celebrated church doorway at Nuremberg, and is especially worthy of notice. On the wall to the right is a doorway leading into the Byzantine Court. This is not copied from any one particular example, but is a composition displaying the elements of the German style. The equestrian statue of St. George is from the Cathedral square at Prague, a work of the 14th century. The seven round bas-reliefs at the top of the doorway, representing scenes from the life of Christ, are fac-simile copies of the originals by Veit Stoss, at the Church of St. Lawrence, in Nuremberg. On either side of this doorway are two monuments, of bishops Siegfrid von Epsteiñ and Peter von Aspelt, opposite to which are the fine monuments of Albert of Saxony, and of Bishop Von Gemmingen ; all of these are cast from the originals, in Mayence Cathedral. Above the arches, and all round the Court, is a small arcade, the capitals, brackets, and other monuments of which are taken from various German churches, but more especially from the Cathedral of Cologne. Immediately over the arches through which we have entered, and between the columns of the arcade, are four bosses with the symbols of the Evangelists, also from Cologne Cathedral.

Passing through the Nuremberg doorway, in the centre, we see immediately before us, and over the arches leading to the nave, eight dancing mummers, from the Town-hall, at Munich ; they are represented as exhibiting before an audience, probably at some civic festival, and are full of grotesque drollery. Beneath the mummers are placed consols or brackets, from the hall of Gurzenich, at Cologne, remarkable for the humour displayed in their conception. On the wall to the right are three large reliefs, from the church of St. Sebald, at Nuremberg. They are the work of Adam Krafft, and represent :—1. The Betrayal of our Saviour ; 2. The Mount of Olives ; 3. The Last Supper ;— and in their execution show great power and much less stiffness than is generally found in mediæval works. Adam Krafft was an excellent sculptor, who flourished at the close of the 15th century. His works, which are chiefly to be found at Nuremberg, possess great merit both in their search after truth and the unusual manual ability they display. Immediately beneath these reliefs is another by the same artist, taken from the Frauen-Kirche, or Church of our Lady, at Nuremberg. It represents an adoration of the Virgin, and shows even more vigorous handling than the other three. On the left hand wall, next to the Nuremberg door, is a bas-relief of "Justice with the Rich and Poor," by Veit Stoss, from the Town-hall, at Nuremberg ; and on the other side of the composition doorway, leading into the English Mediæval Court is the celebrated rose wreath and cross, by Veit Stoss, from Nuremberg, which deserves especial examination as one of the master-pieces of that sculptor, and on account of its very peculiar arrangement. The other subjects found in this Court present excellent examples of German Mediæval Art down to the time of Peter Vischer, whose works evince an evident influence derived from the Renaissance School of Italy, at the close of the 15th and at the commencement of the 16th centuries.

We now emerge into the Nave, and turning to the left, find ourselves in front of

THE ENGLISH MEDIÆVAL COURT.

It will have been remarked in the German Mediæval Court that architecture has undergone another change. No sooner had the Lombard or Romanesque style become systematized, than features arose which contained the germs of yet more important changes.

The Horizontal line principle of antique Art was gradually given up, and a marked inclination towards the Vertical line principle took its place. The full change was yet by no means complete, and it remained for the introduction of the pointed arch in the 12th century, under Norman influence in England and France, to effect a gradual revolution in the whole system of construction and ornamentation, until nearly every trace of the preceding style was lost, and another essentially distinct in all its characteristics arose in its stead:

As we are now standing before the ecclesiastical architecture of our own country, it may be interesting to notice briefly, and in

Entrance to English Mediæval Court.

chronological order, the progress of Pointed architecture in England, and to specify a few of those leading features which serve to distinguish the style of one period from that of another.

Prior to our doing this, it will be well briefly to notice the Norman style which preceded the Pointed, and which was extensively practised by the Normans and English in this country, after the successful invasion by William in 1066. Its leading features are extreme solidity, absence of ornament (at its earliest period), semicircular or horseshoe arches, and the peculiar zigzag mouldings before noted. The buttresses or supports placed against walls to give them strength are broad, but project very little. The pillars are short, massive, and frequently circular, whilst the capitals are usually cubical and channelled in a peculiar manner, sometimes being quite plain, and at others carved with grotesque and symbolic figures and foliage.

The Norman lasted until the 13th century, when it made way for the first pointed style, which is known as *Early*

English. The arches in this style are lancet-shaped ; the pillars consist frequently of small shafts clustering round a circular pier, and are much slighter and taller than the Norman : the capitals are frequently without ornament, being simply plain mouldings. When the capital is carved with foliage the work is boldly executed. Spires too, although originating in the later Norman, rose in the Early English high into the air, like landmarks to the people, to point out where they might congregate to worship their Divine Creator. The buttresses are bold, generally rising in diminishing stages, and either terminating in a triangular head or sloping off into the wall. Windows, two or three in number, were often grouped together under a moulded arch, between the point of which and the tops of the windows an intervening space was formed. This space, pierced with one or more openings, gave rise to that most distinctive and beautiful element of the Gothic style—TRACERY.

The *Decorated* style, which succeeded to the Early English, flourished during the 14th century, and the Court we are now about to enter possesses numerous examples of this, the best and brightest period of English Gothic ; for in the Early English the style had not yet reached its highest point of beauty, and in the later *Perpendicular* it already suffered decline.

Side niche of Tintern door.

Tracery, as we have stated, was the chief characteristic of the Decorated style ; and it consists either of geometrical forms or of flowing lines. As an example of the former, the visitor may examine the arches of the cloister now before us, on the side niche of the Tintern door. The foliated details and carvings, which also give character to this style, may, in like manner, be studied with advantage in this Court. The pillars are either clustered or single, and generally of octangular or circular form ; the capitals are sometimes carved with foliage, at other times they are plain. The buttress is in stages and terminated occasionally with Decorated pinnacles. The execution of the details of this style was admirable, and the variety and beauty of the ornaments, founded chiefly on natural subjects, give to the *Decorated* style an effect which has seldom, if ever, been surpassed.

From the latter part of the 14th to the beginning of the 16th century the *Perpendicular* style was in vogue. It derives its name from the tracery, which instead of taking flowing forms, consists chiefly of vertical lines. The arches became depressed in form, the Tudor arch being distinctive of its later phase, whilst the ornaments were crowded and departed more from natural models. The more important buildings were covered throughout with shallow pannelled work and profuse ornament, over which the eye wanders in vain for much-needed repose, and the effect of breadth and grandeur of parts is lost and frittered away.

These few observations, imperfect as they are, may perhaps assist the visitor's appreciation of the Court we are about to examine. Without further preface, then, we proceed through the archway, as usual, from the Nave.

We are in a cloister of the *Decorated* period, founded in its arches and columns on the Abbey of Guisborough, Yorkshire. Looking through the cloister, to the left, we see before us a doorway from the Chapel of Prince Arthur, son of Henry VII., in Worcester Cathedral, which will enable us to test in a measure the truth of our summary of the Perpendicular style. Crossing the cloister we enter the Mediæval Court, which contains architectural specimens taken from our ancient churches and magnificent cathedrals.

Arcade from Guisborough.

Entering the Court from the Nave, we find, immediately facing us, the magnificent door-way from Rochester Cathedral, coloured so as to give an idea of its appearance when first erected. We may remark here that the practice of colouring and gilding was carried to an almost extravagant extent in the Gothic style, although the effacing hand of Time has left comparatively few examples in a perfect state.

The most remarkable monument on the left of the door, is the richly-decorated Easter sepulchre, from Hawton Church, Nottinghamshire, representing the Resurrection and Ascension of Christ. It was used as an altar; various rites being performed before it, between Good-Friday and Easter-day. Further on in the angle

G

is·a portion of Bishop Alcock's chantry chapel, from Ely Cathedral;
on the other side of the adjoining doorway, which is a composition

Doorway of Rochester Cathedral.

chiefly from the choir of Lincoln Cathedral, we remark the very
beautiful oriel window of John o'Gaunt, at Lincoln, and next to
it a portion of the elaborate altar-screen of Winchester Cathedral.

On the right of the Rochester door is the finely designed monument of Humphrey de Bohun, from Hereford Cathedral, with the
effigy of the knight in complete armour. The door beyond corresponds to the one opposite ; and further on, near the cloister, is
one of the doors of Lichfield Cathedral, with its beautiful iron-
work, the painting of which is remarkably clever ; and a portion

of Bishop Bubwith's monument, from Wells, the door beneath the cloister being from Bishop West's Chapel, Ely. The exquisite niches and canopies round the walls of the court are from Southwell Minster, Ely Cathedral, Beverley Minster, &c. The statues on a line with, and corresponding to those on the monument of Bishop Bubwith, are excellent examples of late Gothic work, from Armagh Cathedral. The upper tier, consisting principally of sculpture, presents valuable examples of that art. The large statues beneath the canopies are from the façade of Wells, and the angels in the spandrels of the arches are from the choir of Lincoln Ca-

Elevation of English Mediæval Court towards the cloister.

a 2

thedral; they are all of the highest interest with reference to the history of sculpture in England. The floor presents a remarkable and interesting series of the best sepulchral monuments of the Gothic period which England possesses, viz., those of Queen Eleanor, from Westminster; Edward II., from Gloucester; the celebrated monument of William of Wykeham, from Winchester; and that of Edward the Black Prince, from Canterbury Cathedral.

Indeed all the subjects in this Court are full of value and interest, and the numerous examples of Gothic art here collected, which we have not space to describe in detail, form a Museum in which the visitor may obtain no inadequate idea of the rich treasures of our country. Passing beneatht he Rochester doorway we enter a vaulted and groined vestibule, the window of which is a beautiful example of the Decorated style, from Holbeach, in Lincolnshire, filled in with rich stained glass. In the centre is the very richly-decorated font, from Walsingham, in Norfolk, an excellent example of the Perpendicular style. The walls of the gallery are lined with statues and monuments; those on the Garden side are all English, principally from the façade of Wells Cathedral; those on the side of the Court are chiefly from Germany and France. Amongst the latter, we draw particular attention to the bas-reliefs on the walls, from Nôtre-Dame, Paris, as excellent examples of early French Gothic. Amongst the central monuments should be particularly remarked the Arderne tomb, from Elford church, Staffordshire; the monument of Henry IV., and Joan of Navarre (his queen), from Canterbury Cathedral; the tomb of Sir Giles Daubeny, from Westminster Abbey, of about the year 1507; and the splendid monument of Richard Beauchamp, Earl of Warwick, from Warwick, one of the finest Gothic sepulchral monuments remaining in England. Passing beneath the arcade, near the Beauchamp monument, we enter

THE FRENCH AND ITALIAN MEDIÆVAL COURT,

On the walls of which, on the ground row, are ranged a series of arches from the choir of Nôtre-Dame, at Paris, the greater number of the canopies which surmount them being taken from the Cathedral of Chartres, both fine examples of early French Gothic art. The very excellent statues, bosses, &c., are from various French churches. The central statue on the floor is by the great Italian sculptor, Giovanni Pisano (13th century), and stands on a pedestal from the celebrated altar-piece of Or San Michele, at Florence, by Andrea Orgagna (14th century). The two statues nearest the gallery are by Nino Pisano, son of Giovanni. The very elaborate example of iron-work near the nave entrance is from one of the great west doors of the Cathedral of Nôtre-Dame, Paris, and evinces such consummate skill in workmanship as to have obtained for its artist, when first made public, the unenviable credit of being in close league with the Evil One. The exact date of this iron-work is not ascertained, but it is of the best period of the French Pointed style.

Once more regaining the Nave, we proceed on our journey southward, until a few steps bring us to

THE RENAISSANCE COURT.

Man had wrought for centuries patiently and laboriously at Gothic architecture, and had advanced, by regular stages, to the perfection of that style, which, after reaching its zenith in the 14th century, as regularly and decidedly declined in excellence, until the indispensable principles of true art—simplicity, and good taste—were, towards the close of the 15th century, overwhelmed by excess of ornament. Whilst this downward road was followed by most European artists, various causes led to the revival of the Antique in Italy, and at the commencement of the 15th century, the celebrated Brunelleschi produced a work founded on the Antique Roman style, of the highest merit, viz., the Dome of Florence Cathedral. In the year 1420, Ghiberti executed his wonderful bronze doors, and from thenceforward the new style of the revived art, or the Renaissance, as it is now usually called, advanced rapidly, first throughout Italy, and, in the succeeding century, throughout Europe. Amongst the causes which led to this revival may be included the decline of the feudal system, the growing freedom of thought, the recent discoveries of the New World, and of the art of Printing. With the rise of the spirit of personal independence was created a thirst for ancient literature and art, and a search for the hidden fountains of antiquity was enthusiastically persevered in, until in the end it proved eminently successful.

Monastic libraries, in obedience to the demands of the public voice, yielded up their treasures of ancient literature, whilst the soil of Italy was made to disgorge its mutilated fragments of antique art. The effects of these sudden, unexpected, and precious acquisitions may readily be imagined; they created a complete revolution in literature and art throughout Italy, which spread thence into other countries. The two beautiful arts of Painting and Sculpture saw with emulative shame their present inferiority in the ranks of Art; and in their noble aspirations towards the perfection newly placed before them, they assumed their position as distinct and legitimate creations. But if the Gothic system was now dying out, it had left at least one valuable legacy to the future, in its appreciation and adoption of natural models. The Italian artists of the 15th century received the gift joyfully, and, combining it with what treasures antiquity afforded them, produced a style which, in sculpture especially, has all the freshness of nature and the refinement of the antique, as both were capable of being united by gifted men whose names have come down in glory to our own day, and will command the admiration of the latest posterity.

On no branch of art did the revival of the antique more strongly act, than on the art of architecture; the Gothic style, which had never taken deep root in the soil of classic Italy, speedily fell altogether in that country before the recent discovery and imitation of the Roman antiquities. No powerful body of Freemasons was there, as in England, France, and Germany, to oppose the

progress of the new style; and the individual energy of such men as Brunelleschi, Bramante, and the great architects of the northern states, soon established it on an indestructible basis. And, however much a partizan spirit may decry this or that particular style, the productions influenced by the revival of the antique, throughout the 15th century, especially in architecture and sculpture, will never fail to excite our astonishment and emulation.

The façade before us is a restored copy of a portion of the Hôtel Bourgtheroulde, at Rouen.

Arcade of Hôtel Bourgtheroulde at Rouen.

It was built at the end of the 15th and the beginning of the 16th centuries. The bas-relief before us represents the Field of the Cloth of Gold, and the memorable meeting (in 1520) of Francis I. of France and our own

Henry VIII. The frieze above is from the Hospital of the Poor, at Pistoia, in Tuscany, and shows monks or priests relieving the poor; the original is in coloured porcelain. Entering the Court, we find in the lunettes under the ceiling of the small loggia, or gallery, portraits of twelve of the most celebrated persons of Italy, Spain, France, and Germany, of the Renaissance period, including in the central compartment Francis I. of France, and Catharine de' Medici. In the compartment to the right are, Lorenzo de' Medici and Lucrezia Borgia; and, in that to the left, Mary of Burgundy and Maximilian of Germany. In the centre of the Court we find a fountain of the Renaissance period, from the Château de Gaillon, in France; and on either side of the fountain are two bronze wells, from the Ducal Palace at Venice. Directing our steps to the right, we may first examine the decorations on the lower part of the interior of the façade, the bas-relief of which is taken from the high altar at Granada Cathedral, in Spain. The statue in the centre is that of the wife of Louis de Poncher, the original of which is now in the Louvre; its date may be assigned to the early portion of the 16th century. The altar on which the statue is placed is from the Certosa near Pavia, in Northern Italy. The first object on the side-wall is a door, by Jean Goujon (a French sculptor who executed many works at the Louvre), from the church of Saint Maclou, at Rouen; then a doorway from the Doria Palace at Genoa, a fine specimen of the cinque-cento; above this are five bas-reliefs from the museum at Florence, representing Faith, Prayer, Wisdom, Justice, and Charity; and beyond it, one of the most beautiful objects in the palace, a copy of the far-famed gates from the Baptistery at Florence, executed by Lorenzo Ghiberti, who was occupied upon his work for the space of twenty-one years. One glance is sufficient to assure the spectator that sculpture had indeed advanced to an extraordinary degree of excellence at the period which we have now reached. The visitor having sufficiently admired these " Gates of Paradise," as Michael Angelo termed them, will proceed on his way, passing another doorway, which, like that on the other side, already seen, is from Genoa. Close to it, is a door by Goujon, corresponding to the door in the opposite corner.

On the back wall we first notice a composition made up from various examples of cinque-cento work. Adjoining it is a portion of an altar from the Certosa, near Pavia,—a beautiful specimen of sculptural art of the time. Next to this is another piece of cinque-cento composition, from specimens at the same Certosa, from Rouen Cathedral and other places. In the centre, two colossal figures (Caryatides), from the Louvre, by Jean Goujon, support a large cast of the Nymph of Fontainebleau, by the celebrated Benvenuto Cellini. Next to the Caryatides we see an exquisite specimen of a portion of the interior of the principal entrance to the Certosa most elaborately carved, and the panels filled in with bas-reliefs ; the doorway by its side is from the Hôtel de Ville, of Oudenarde, in Belgium. It stands out from the wall, and looks very like an antique cabinet or screen. Another architectural example from the Certosa follows, being a sort of military monument erected to the memory of G. G. Visconti, Duke of Milan ; the date of its execution is the end of the 15th century. On the side next the French Mediæval Court is first another oak door from Saint Maclou by Jean Goujon, and then a doorway, from Genoa ; and, above it, the frieze of " The Singers," by Luca della Robbia, the original of which is at Florence, a most charming work, full of life and animation. In the centre of this—the northern—side of the Court, is a cast from one of the windows of the façade of the Certosa, a remarkably fine example of cinque-cento ; next to it, another doorway, from the Doria Palace at Genoa ; and in the corner a fourth door from Saint Maclou, by Goujon, the central bas-relief of which represents the Baptism of Christ. The lower part of the interior of the façade is devoted to examples of Italian sculpture of the 15th century, including a head of St. John by Donatello.

The monument placed against the wall is that of Ilaria di Caretto, from Lucca Cathedral, executed by Jacopo della Quercia, of Sienna, early in the 15th century : it is a very fine example of the cinque-cento style.

Two statues by Donatello cannot fail to be noticed—his St. John and David, which display great power and study of nature.

We now pass out through the doorway under the Nymph of Fontainebleau, and enter a vestibule in the Renaissance style. Here, on the ceiling, is a copy of a painting from the Sala del Cambio (Exchange) at Perugia, in Italy, by Perugino, the master of Raffaelle, who assisted Perugino in the work. The painting represents the Seven Planets, with Apollo in the centre, as the personification of the Sun. The wall of the Renaissance Court to the left of the entrance is decorated with terra-cotta arches, and a frieze from the Certosa ; the singing boys in the frieze are of great merit. The bronze monument in the centre is that of Lewis of Bavaria, a very interesting example of late German

Gothic, remarkable for the finish of its details. On either side of the doorway are parts of Goujon's doors from St. Maclou, at Rouen. In the centre of the gallery are placed Germain Pilon's "Graces," now in the Louvre, a charming example of the French school of sculpture. The four angles under the Perugia ceiling are occupied by four statues, also by Pilon; and the very remarkable bronze effigy in the centre, against the garden, is from the Museum at Florence; it is ascribed to Vecchietta of Sienna.

The kneeling effigies in the gallery are from the Hertford monument in Salisbury Cathedral, probably erected in the first half of the 17th century. On the back wall, to the right of the doorway, are richly ornamented arches in terra-cotta, from the large cloisters of the Certosa, and also bas-reliefs and specimens of the Renaissance style from various parts of Italy. The central monument of Bernard von Gablenz is an exceedingly fine example of the style as practised in Germany, at the close of the 16th century. After examining these objects, we turn into the narrow court adjoining the Renaissance Court, and find ourselves in

Façade from Elizabethan Court.

THE ELIZABETHAN COURT.

The architectural details in this Court are taken from Holland House, at Kensington, a fine old mansion made interesting to us by many associations. Elizabethan architecture, which was in its

flower during the latter half of the 16th century—more than a
hundred years after the revival of classical architecture in Italy—
shows the first symptoms of the adoption of the new style in
England. The Elizabethan style—the name reaches back over the
century—is characterized by a rough imitation of antique detail
applied to masses of building, in which many Gothic features
were still retained as regards general form, but altered as to ornament. The style being in its very nature transitory, it gradually
gave way, although characterized by a certain palatial grandeur and
striking picturesqueness, before the increasing knowledge which
England obtained of Italian architecture, until we find it entirely
displaced in the first half of the 17th century by the excellent
style of building introduced by Inigo Jones. We must add, that,
although it has no pretensions to the character of a regular or
complete system, yet few who have visited the great Elizabethan
mansions scattered over England can have failed to admire their
picturesque and solid appearance, their stately halls, corridors,
staircases, and chimney-pieces, and the beautiful garden terraces,
which form so important a feature in their general design.

This Court contains several tombs of the period. The first is
that of Sir John Cheney, from Salisbury Cathedral : a soldier who
distinguished himself in the wars of the Roses, and was attached
to the party of Henry VII. The original effigy is in alabaster,
a material much used during the early part of the 16th century.
The next monument is that of Mary Queen of Scots from Westminster Abbey, executed in the beginning of the 17th century,
and displaying in its treatment all the characteristics of the Elizabethan style. The succeeding monument is that of Queen
Elizabeth, also from Westminster, constructed at about the same
period as that of Queen Mary ; the original effigy is of white
marble. The last monument is that of Margaret, Countess of
Richmond and Derby (the mother of Henry VII.), at Westminster.
It is the work of the Florentine sculptor Torrigiano ; the original
is in copper, and its date the early part of the 16th century ; it
is of unusual merit. Advancing a few paces, the visitor again
reaches the Nave, and turning still southward, finds himself before

The Italian Court.

THE ITALIAN COURT:

Which, as will be at once remarked, closely resembles the style of antique Roman art, on which, indeed, the modern is professedly founded. Although Brunelleschi, as we have before observed, revived the practice of antique architecture as early as the year 1420, yet various causes combined to delay a thorough investigation of the antique remains until the close of the century ; and it even is not until the commencement of the 16th century that we find the Italian style, or modernized Roman, regularly systematized and generally received throughout Italy ; from whence it gradually extended, first to Spain and to France, and at a somewhat later period into England and Germany. The power and excellence of the style are nobly exhibited in a large number of buildings, amongst which may be noted the ancient Library at Venice, St. Peter's at Rome, the Pitti Palace, Florence, the Basilica of Vicenza, the great Colonnade of the Louvre, Paris ; St. Paul's Cathedral, London ; and the Escurial Palace, near Madrid.

In this style, architecture rests chiefly on its own intrinsic excellence, or on proportion, symmetry, and good taste. The arts of sculpture and painting, in a great measure, become independent of architecture ; and their absence in buildings of a later period (the 17th and 18th centuries, for instance) led to a coldness of character, which happily promises at the present day to find its remedy.

The Court before which we stand is founded on a portion of the finest palatial edifice in Rome,—the Farnese Palace, commenced by the architect Antonio Sangallo, for Cardinal Farnese, and finished under the direction of Michael Angelo. A curious fact in connexion with the original building is, that the stones which compose it were taken from the ancient Coliseum, within whose mighty walls the early Christians suffered martyrdom ; so that, in truth, the same stones which bore witness to the faith and courage of the early devotees, served afterwards to build, for the faith triumphant a palace in which luxury, worldliness, and pride, found a genial home.

Prior to entering the Court, we may remark, in the niches, the bronze statues by Sansovino, from the Campanile Loggia at Venice, amongst which Apollo is conceived quite in the old Roman spirit. Passing beneath the columns in the centre of the court, we see the fountain of the Tartarughe, or "of the Tortoises" at Rome, designed by Giacomo della Porta, with bronze statues by Taddeo Landini. Turning to the right, the first object that attracts our attention is a statue of the Virgin and Child, by Michael Angelo, the original of which is at San Lorenzo, Florence. Advancing to the south side, we enter a loggia or arcade, the interior of which is richly ornamented with copies of Raffaelle's celebrated frescoes in the Loggie of the Vatican palace at Rome. They consist of a most fanciful, yet tasteful, combination of landscape figures, architecture and foliage, founded on antique models, and bearing a close resemblance to the ornamental work discovered in various Roman ruins, especially at the towns of Pompeii and Herculaneum, which, however, were at that time unknown. In the centre of the arcade, towards the Court, is the monument of Giuliano de' Medici, from San Lorenzo, Florence. On each side of his statue are the reclining figures Night and Light (part of the same monument). This is one of Michael Angelo's masterpieces, and is remarkably characteristic of the sculptor's style. At the back of it, in the Loggia, is a fine specimen of bronze casting, from Venice. On each side of the entrance to the gallery are two groups of a Virgin with the dead Christ, that to the right being by Bernini, the other to the left by Michael Angelo, both especially interesting as serving to indicate the state of art in the 16th and 17th centuries respectively. The remaining statues, as far as the loggia, are by Michael Angelo. The visitor may now enter the loggia, which, like its companion on the other side of the Court, is ornamented with copies of Raffaelle's frescoes from the Vatican ; in the centre of this side of the Court is placed Michael Angelo's celebrated monument of Lorenzo de' Medici, from the church of San Lorenzo at Florence ; the reclining figures on each side of the statue of Lorenzo represent Dawn and Twilight. At the back of this monument within the arcade is the fine bronze door by Sansovino from St. Mark's, Venice, on which he is said to have laboured from twenty to thirty years. .The projecting heads are supposed to be portraits ; amongst them are those of Titian, Aretino, and of the sculptor himself. Proceeding onwards, the beautiful composition of Jonah and the Whale, by Raffaelle, is from the Chigi Chapel at Rome. Passing into the gallery on the Garden side, we remark in the four angles the pedestals of the Venetian standards, from the Square of St. Mark, Venice. The painted ceilings of this gallery deserve especial attention. The first on entering the gallery is from an existing example at the " Old Library," Venice ; the last is from the " Camera della Segnatura," by Raffaelle, at the Vatican ; beneath which is the fine statue of St. Jerome, by Torrigiano, from Seville, in Spain.

The monuments on the external wall of the vestibule afford excellent examples of the later Renaissance style. Amongst them may be particularly noted the monument of Lancinio Curzio (nearest the gallery), from Milan, by Agostino Busti, evincing that delicate execution for which the sculptor was famous ; and the central altar of La Madonna della Scarpa, from the Cathedral of St. Mark, Venice—an elaborate specimen of bronze casting, completed early in the 16th century by Pietro Lombardo and others. The monument on the side nearest the Nave is an excellent example of the Renaissance style.

The decoration of the vestibule is founded on the very elegant Casa Taverna at Milan, by Bernardino Luini, a pupil of Leonardo da Vinci, and affords an excellent idea of the peculiar painted mural ornament prevailing in Italy at the commencement of the 16th century. The doors are from the Palace of the Cancellaria at Rome, by Bramante, the famous designer of St. Peter's in that city, and the immediate predecessor of the great architects of the 16th century. The vestibule itself is rich in very beautiful drawings after the old masters, by Mr. West.

We have now completed our survey of one of the most interesting features of the Crystal Palace. We have performed our promise to guide the visitor through the various Fine Art Courts, bringing before his notice some of the principal objects that have

adorned his road, and endeavouring, by our brief remarks, to
heighten the pleasure he must necessarily have experienced from

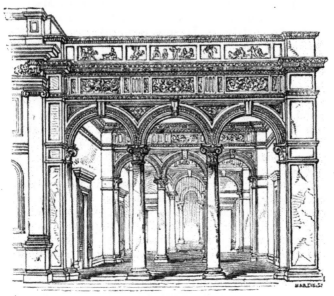

Façade of Italian Vestibule.

the sight of so noble an assemblage of architectural and sculptural
art. Much however remains to be seen and accomplished—much
that requires patient examination and study—examination that
will yield fresh beauty, and study that will be rewarded by permanent and useful knowledge. For guidance and help we refer
the visitor to the handbooks of the several Courts. The mission of

Frieze of Italian Court.

this little work, as far as the Fine Art Courts are concerned, is accomplished : and "THE GUIDE BOOK" now only waits until the visitor has sufficiently recovered from his fatigue, in order to resume, in other parts of the building, the part of cicerone.

Crossing the great transept to the west, we proceed towards the south end of the building, and, keeping to the right hand, commence our pilgrimage through the Industrial Courts. The first that we arrive at is

THE STATIONERY COURT.

In the formation of this and of the other Industrial Courts, the several architects have been solicitous to express, both in the construction and the decoration, as far as possible, the specific destination : with the view of maintaining some harmony between the objects exhibited and the building in which they are contained. The Stationery Court has been designed and erected by Mr. J. G. Crace. The style of this Court is composite, and may be regarded as the application of cinque-cento ornamental decoration to a wooden structure. Externally the aim has been to furnish certain coloured surfaces, which shall harmonize with the plants around and with the general aspect of the Palace. In the interior of the Court, the dark neutral tint on the lower level will be seen to serve as an admirable background to the objects exhibited ; whilst the panels covered with cinque-cento decoration, combined with the elegant imitation of marquetrie work, produce an effect which deserves the highest praise. Over the opening through which we enter this Court, and between the stained glass windows let into the wall, have been introduced allegorical figures of the arts and sciences applied in the manufacture of the articles exhibited in the Court, and over the opening at the back the artist has depicted the *Genii* of Manufacture, Commerce, &c. In the centre of the panels throughout the Court representations are painted of the processes which the objects exhibited undergo during their manufacture.

As the visitor passes round this Court, let him step out at one of the entrances on the north side, close to which he will find erected "THE CRYSTAL PALACE MEDAL PRESS." This machine, which is official, and worked on behalf of the Company by Messrs. T. R. Pinches and Co., will be employed from time to time in striking commemorative medals, designed by Mr. Pinches or other artists connected with the Palace. The machine is worked by four men, one of whom adjusts the metal to be stamped between the sunk

dies : as soon as the metal is fixed, the other workmen swing the
lever rapidly round, and the great pressure produces impressions of
the dies on the metal, which is turned out sharp and distinct, and
then put into a lathe and completed.   In the glass cases placed
near, the visitor will have an opportunity of inspecting numerous
specimens of the medals produced by the machine, amongst which
those in frosted silver deserve especial notice for the beauty of
their appearance.

The visitor, proceeding round the Stationery Court, from, right
to left, will find amongst the works of industry exhibited, fancy
stationery, books, specimens of ornamental printing, pencil
drawings, and other articles of the kind.   At the back of this and
of the Birmingham Court, or towards the west front of the
building, is situated "THE HARDWARE COURT," in which are
placed household utensils, iron and zinc bronzes, gas-fittings,
refrigerators, and numerous articles in metals.   At the back of this
Court again, is a large space extending in a southerly direction from
the Hardware Court to the Pompeian Court (at which the visitor
will presently arrive), devoted to the exhibition of furniture.
Here will be found not only useful articles of household furniture,
but specimens of tapestry work, wood carving, picture frames, and
other ornamental articles which give grace to our rooms, and
which, by means of our great mechanical excellence, are daily
becoming more and more within the reach of the great body of the
people.   The visitor will do well, in examining these Courts, to view
them in sections, so as not to miss those Industrial Courts which
face the Nave.   Emerging from the opening that leads to the south
side of the Stationery Court, a few steps will bring him once more
into the Nave, where he will notice a stand appropriated to the
exhibition and printing by the Messrs. Day, of chromo-lithographic
views of some of the most picturesque and interesting portions of the
contents of the Crystal Palace.   These coloured views are produced
by Mr. P. H. Delamotte, and they gain an additional interest from
the fact, that the process of printing is witnessed by the visitor in
the Palace.   The greatest accuracy is obtained in fixing the colours
by means of the registring process.

Next in order of the Industrial establishments, comes

THE BIRMINGHAM COURT.

This Court has been designed by Mr. Tite, and the architect has
considered that the purpose to which the Court is applied might

best be expressed by showing some of the principal ornamental uses of iron in architecture. With this intention, he has designed for the façade of the court a restoration, in modern work, of the English ornamental iron enclosures of the 17th century, which differed but slightly from those prevailing at the same time in France in the style of Louis XIV. The English, however, are generally richer in foliage, while the latter are more fanciful in scroll work. At the period referred to, the whole of those enclosures were of wrought and hammered iron, cast-iron being at that time little known, but in the enclosure before us, although it has been executed on much the same principle as the old work, the ornaments are cast, in order to secure greater durability, cast-iron not being so easily destroyed as wrought-iron, by the oxidation which proceeds with such enormous rapidity in this country. The castings have been most admirably executed, and so sharp and distinct were the outlines of the patterns, that they required but little after-finishing. The pilasters are of enamelled slate, excellent for their imitation of marble, surmounted by iron capitals. Entering through the gates in the centre, the visitor finds the interior of the court panelled in the style of the same period and decorated by Mr. Sang with emblematical paintings and other appropriate ornamentation in encaustic.

In this court will be found articles in nickel silver, seal-presses, gilt toys, metallic bedsteads, and similar manufactured goods of universal use. Quitting this department, we approach the next Industrial Court in succession,

THE SHEFFIELD COURT.

The architect of this court is Mr. G. H. Stokes, whose structure at once compels attention by the novelty of its design, and by its general striking effect. Although there is a considerable admixture of styles in the court, the parts have been so well selected and their blending is so excellently contrived, that they yield a harmonious result in every way pleasing to the eye. The materials used in the construction are plate-glass and iron, an appropriate and happy selection for a court intended to receive the productions of Sheffield. The panels on the outer walls are of plate-glass, inclosed within gilt-mouldings; the pilasters and the frieze over the large panels are likewise of plate-glass. The iron columns above, forming an arcade, are in a composite Moresque-Gothic style, and elaborately ornamental in design. Entering the court

H

from the nave, we find the interior decorations identical with those of the exterior—with two differences, viz., the large lower panels, instead of being of plate-glass, are of red cloth, which serves as a back ground to throw up and display the articles exhibited. The frieze or space above the columns, now merely covered with painted decorations, will, at a future period be adorned with paintings, illustrative of the manufacture of Sheffield ware.

Leading out of this department will be found, at the back, a space devoted to mineral manufactures, including works of art in terra-cotta, tiles, marble, and glass, &c. Having made our way to the nave, a step brings us at once before the exquisite restoration of

The Bay and City of Naples.

THE POMPEIAN COURT.

Seventeen hundred and seventy-five years ago, the cities of Herculaneum and Pompeii, beautifully situated on the shores of the Bay of Naples, were buried beneath the cinders and ashes vomited forth by Vesuvius. The horrors of this calamity are recorded in the writings of Pliny, and of other Roman historians of the period. So sudden was the outbreak and general convulsion that, as we learn, many of the inhabitants of those cities were caught in their terrible doom before the thought of

THE POMPEIAN COURT.

H 2

escape occurred to them. The dread event completed, nature resumed her former aspect. The mountain flames ceased, the intense blue sky again looked down upon the dancing waters, and there was nothing to tell of the general havoc, but a vast desolate tract covered with white ashes, under which man and his works lay entombed.

For upwards of sixteen hundred years the cities continued undisturbed beneath their crust. But about the middle of the last century, curiosity with respect to them was stirred, inquiry commenced, and excavations were attempted. As in the more recent case of Nineveh, but with still more satisfactory results, success at once crowned investigation. The material that had destroyed Herculaneum and Pompeii had also preserved them. That which had robbed them of life had also perpetuated their story in death. The cities were redelivered to man so far undecayed, that he obtained actual visible knowledge of the manner of life of one of the most remarkable people that ever governed the world. To the insight thus obtained, the visitor is indebted for the reproduction of the Pompeian house before which he now stands—a habitation of the time, complete in every respect, from the outer walls to the most insignificant object in domestic use.

The doorway of this house stands fronting the nave. Entering it, we pass through the narrow prothyrum or passage, on either side of which is a room devoted to the door-keeper and slaves, and on its pavement the words " *cave canem*,"—beware of the dog—meet the eye. It is the usual notice engraved on the threshold of these Roman houses. Emerging from the passage, we are at once in the " *atrium*," or outer hall of the edifice. The eye is not attracted here, as in other restorations of the palace, by the architectural design alone; the attention is also secured and charmed by the decorations. The bright coloured walls, the light, fanciful character of the ornaments, the variety of patterns, and the excellent method of colouring, which at the lower part is dark, and graduates upwards, until it becomes white on the ceiling—constitute some of the beautiful features that give individuality to Pompeian houses, and cause them to differ most essentially from every other style.

This entire hall, or " *atrium*," was the part of the building common to all visitors. The opening above is the " *compluvium*," and the marble basin beneath, the " *impluvium*," which received the rain that fell from the roof. In the actual houses at Pompeii, the size of the " *impluvium*" corresponds, of course, with the dimensions of the opening above. Here the " *compluvium*" has been widened in order to admit more light into the court. The flooring consists of tesselated pavement, and near the two other doorways leading into the "*atrium*," is inscribed the well known word "Salve"—"welcome"—announcing the profuse hospitality of the owner. Two out of the three entrances mentioned are formed here for convenience of egress and ingress, and are not copied from actual buildings, in which only one door exists.

As soon as we have entered the court, we turn to the right, and proceed round it, stepping into the "*cubicula*," or bed chambers, to admire the figures that seem to be suspended in the intensely fine atmosphere, and—with our English experiences—to wonder how, whether by day or by night, comfort could be attained in such close dormitories. We reach the side entrance, next to which is an open recess corresponding with a second recess on the other side of the "*atrium*." These recesses were called "*alæ*," or wings, and were used for the transaction of business with visitors. On the central panel of the first recess is painted a scene from the story of "Perseus and Andromeda," and on the side panel are again exquisite figures, painted not in the centre of the panel, producing a stiff formality, but nearer to the top than to the bottom, so that the forms still seem to float before us. Continuing our way, we turn into the large apartment opposite the door at which we entered. This is the "*tablinum*," and was used for the reception of the family archives, pictures, and objects of art. It probably served the purposes also of the modern "drawing-room." Across the "*tablinum*" a curtain was no doubt drawn, to separate the private dwelling-house from the more public "*atrium*," although it is a remarkable fact that no remains of hooks or rings, or of anything else, has been discovered to convey an idea of the means by which such a curtain could be attached. In order to enter within the "*tablinum*" a special invitation was required.

From this point, the "Peristyle" is also visible, with its columns coloured red some way up, a flower garden in the centre, and a back wall, upon which are curious specimens of perspective decoration, in which the Romans seem to have delighted. This court was always open to the sky in the middle. Passing through the "*tablinum*" and turning to the right, we come to a small doorway which admits us into the "*triclinium*," or dining-room. The Roman dining-room generally contained three couches, each large enough to hold three persons. In feeding, the Roman was accustomed to lie on his breast and to stretch out his hand towards the table in order to serve himself. When dinner was over, he turned

on his left side, and leant on his elbow.   Re-entering the Peristyle,
we proceed on our way, still to the right, and pass a drinking-
room, on the walls of which fruits are painted, some hanging in
golden clusters on a wreath of foliage, supported by Cupids.   Next
to this is the "*porta postica,*" or back door, and, adjoining it a
small recess, which served as kitchen.   Crossing the "Peristyle,"
near one end of which is the domestic altar, we turn to the left,
and, after passing a small chamber, reach the bath-room—that
chamber so essential to the luxurious Roman.   Close to this
is the summer dining-room, and beyond this again, and corresponding with the "*triclinium,*" is the bed-chamber of the mistress
of the house.   Quitting this, we once more gain the "*atrium,*"
by means of narrow *fauces,* or passages, and return to the nave,
through the door of the house at which we originally entered.   The
visitor has seen the extremes of decorative art, when, after sating
his eyes with the profuse and dazzling embellishment of the
Alhambra, he has also dwelt upon the delicate work of colours
gracing the walls of Pompeii.

View of Vesuvius, between Castellamare and Gragnano.

ETHNOLOGICAL AND NATURAL HISTORY DEPARTMENT.

Upon quitting the Pompeian Court the visiter, still walking south-wards, crosses the south transept and enters that division of the building which is devoted to geographical groupings of men, animals, and plants. The illustrations of the animal and vegetable kingdoms in the Crystal Palace have been arranged upon a specific principle and plan. Although the British Museum contains nearly all the examples of animals and birds known in the world, and Kew Gardens exhibit specimens of the majority of trees and plants known to botanists—still neither of these collections affords the visiter any accurate idea of the manner in which these numerous objects are scattered over the earth. Nor do they assist his conjectures as to the nature or the general aspect of their native countries. Here an attempt has been made to remove the confusion; and it is believed that the associations of these two branches of Natural Science, in groupings arranged in such a manner as the nature of the building will permit, coupled with illustrations of the human variety belonging to the same soil (a collection which has never before been attempted in any country) will prove both instructive and amusing, and afford a clearer conception than can be obtained elsewhere of the manner in which the varieties of man, animals, and plants, are distributed over the globe.

Zoology (from *Zoön*, an animal,) is, strictly speaking, that science which investigates the whole animal kingdom, comprehending man as well as the inferior animals. Zoology therefore, in a wide sense, includes Ethnology, or so much of that science as considers the different varieties or races of men in a physical point of view, instituting comparisons between them, and carefully pointing out the differences or affinities which characterize the physical structure of various branches of the great human family. In more confined use, the term zoology relates only to the consideration and study of the mammalia, or warm-blooded animals; the requirements of scientific research having occasioned a new nomenclature in order to distinguish the different branches of the same study. Hence the natural history of birds is particularized as Ornithology, and that of fish, as Ichthyology, whilst the investigation of those characters in man which serve to distinguish one race from another is, as previously remarked, called Ethnology (from the Greek *Ethnos*, "nation"). This last-named science is subdivided again into different branches, but, in a limited and inferior sense, and as illustrated by the various groups in the Palace,

it may be described as that science which distinguishes the
differences in skin, hair, bone, and stature that exist between the
various races of men.   This zoological branch of Ethnology relates
to the physical history of man as opposed to his mental history,
and following up the course of his wanderings, endeavours by
the above-mentioned physical peculiarities to ascend to the source
from which the several migrating races have proceeded.

Within the Palace itself, we have been enabled to remark the
works of man, and the gradual development of his ideas, especially
in Art, leading to a variety of so-called "styles," which answer in
a measure to the varied *species* of Divinely created life.   We have
now an opportunity of attentively considering the more marvellous
and infinite creations of the Deity in the organization and development of that greatest of all mysteries—life itself; and of obtaining
a vivid idea of those peculiar varieties of mankind, that have
hitherto not fallen under our personal observation.   If the visitor
should feel astonishment in the presence of some of the phases of
human existence here presented to him, he may do well to bear
in mind, that they are representations of human beings endowed
with immortal souls ; to whose capabilities we may not place a
limit, and that it is not yet two thousand years since the forefathers of the present European family tattooed their skins, and
lived in so savage a state, that late archæological researches
induce us to suspect they were not wholly free from one of the
worst charges that is laid to savage existence ; viz. the practice of
cannibalism.*

Entering upon the path immediately before him, the visitor will
commence the examination of the groups arranged on the western
side of the nave which illustrate the Ethnology, Zoology, and
Botany of

THE NEW WORLD.

The first section we come to is devoted to the illustration of the
Arctic regions : to the left on entering are placed two polar bears ;
the skin of the largest having been brought home by Captain
Inglefield on his last memorable return from the Arctic regions.
The smaller bear died in England some years ago.   To the right
will be found a group of Esquimaux, a race of people inhabiting
the ice-bound shores of the Arctic regions, and who from the nature
of their language, and the position of their country, are comparatively isolated from the rest of mankind.   They pass their short

* Archæol. Journ., p. 207. Sept. 1853.

summers in hunting foxes and fishing, and during the winter, form dwelling-places in the frozen snow ; their principal means of subsistence being, during that season, dried fish, and whale oil. They are short of stature, possess broad faces, resembling in some respects the Chinese, straight long hair, and well-proportioned limbs, and are generally plump and even fat. Since the introduction of Christianity amongst the Esquimaux, they have advanced in civilization. Continuing along the path, we pass a glass-case containing a selection of North American birds, and beyond this we arrive at a group of North American Red Indians engaged in a war-dance, and surrounded by the trees and shrubs indigenous to North America. The most conspicuous amongst these are the American Rhododendrons, the Kalmias, the Andromedas, and the American *arbor vitæ*. The Indians of the valley of the Mississippi, and of the *drainage* of the Great Lakes supply us with our current ideas of the so-called Red Man, or the Indian of the New World. In stature they are above the middle height, and exhibit great muscular force, their powers of endurance being very great ; in temper they are harsh, stoical, and unsociable, whilst in warfare they are savage and cruel. The general physiognomy of the Red Indians is the same from the Rocky Mountains to the Atlantic. Between the Alleghanies and the Atlantic, the first-known country of these tribes, the variety is now nearly extinct.

Quitting this group and continuing our way, the visitor finds before him a glass tank containing some of the North American fluviatile (river) animals, such as the bull frog and snapping turtle, and on his right a case of West Indian marine objects, exhibited in order to afford an idea of the nature of the sea bottom in that region. In this case are mollusques, corals, sponges, &c. This rare collection of objects is the property of J. S. Boworbank, Esq., by whom they have been kindly lent to the Crystal Palace, and arranged.

Returning a short distance, and taking the left-hand path, we find on our right the trees and animals of Central America ; amongst the latter a fine male puma grey with age. Before reaching this, the visitor will note a large specimen of *Agave Americana*, one of the most striking plants of Central America. The puma may be regarded as the American representative of the lion of the old world, the distribution of both these animals throughout their respective hemispheres having originally been very general. Like most of the cat tribe the puma is a good climber, and usually chooses trees, rocks, and other elevated

positions from which it can dart upon its prey. On the left of
the visitor are two groups, representative of the North Brazils.
The greatest group on the left hand is characteristic of Guiana, and
beyond it is the Amazonian group. These two are intended to serve
as types of the South American varieties of Indians. And if we
institute a comparison between the various races of North and South
America, it will be found that the latter possess more delicate
features, rounder forms, and are of smaller stature. Their habits
and pursuits also differ. The red Indian of North America gives
himself up entirely to hunting, whilst the South American
devotes his life to fishing, guiding his light canoe down the
rapid rolling rivers of his country, in search of the means of subsistence.

Continuing our path, we arrive at a case of South American
birds, and, beyond this, a zoological group. On the ground, to the
left, is a jaguar, which has just killed a brocket deer, and is about
to eat it, when his repast is disturbed by a growl from a black
jaguar, who is coming down the rocks, on the right, to contest the
prey with his spotted brother. As the leopard is found only in
the old world, so is the jaguar met with in the New World only,
and each may be regarded as a representative of the other, on
opposite sides of the Atlantic ocean ; the jaguar having greatly the
advantage in size and muscular strength. Near these is placed an
adult and a young specimen of the llama, or guanaco, as it is
called by the Peruvians, who employ this animal as a beast of
burden, notwithstanding its small size and apparent inability to
sustain heavy loads. Like the dromedary, it is capable of enduring
great fatigue, and can climb over almost impassable roads. Indeed,
until the introduction of mules and horses by the Spaniards, these
little creatures brought to the sea-side all the gold and silver from
the world-famous mines of the Andes.

Leaving this episode of wild animal life, the visitor advances on
his path, and, after passing a case of birds, arrives at another
group of animals, illustrative of South America. Amongst these
will be seen a specimen of the tapir, of which there are but three
kinds, this (the American) being not only the largest of the three,
but also the largest native animal of South America. It is of a
harmless and timid nature, living on vegetable food, and shunning
the haunts of man. It appears intermediate in form between
the hog and the elephant, and may be regarded as the New
World representative of the latter, amongst thick-skinned animals.

Next to this is a puma, about to spring upon a brocket-deer, whose shoulders it would seize, and whom it would destroy by pulling back the head with its paws, until it would break the little creature's neck.   The ethnological group, on the right, is a representation of a party of Botocudos, two of whom are engaged in a fierce fight with sticks.   These inhabitants of South America are regarded as the fiercest of American savages ; they are yellow in colour, their hair is long and lank, their eyes are small, their cheek bones prominent, the expression of their coun-

The Tapir.

tenance is excessively savage, and they give themselves a still wilder appearance by the introduction of blocks of hard wood in the under-lip, and in the ears.   Missionary efforts, it is consolatory to think, have done something towards civilizing these savages, who have been induced to become industrious and to turn their attention to the cultivation of the soil.   Owing to the tropical character of the regions to which the foregoing groups of South American men and animals belong, the botanical specimens are not large.   Nevertheless, the species introduced are strictly correct. They consist, principally, of Brugmansias, Fuchsias, Calceolarias, and those two splendid members of the fir tribe, *Araucaria imbricata* and *Braziliana.*

Such are the first specimens presented, in the Crystal Palace, of the zoological and other curiosities of the New World. Others in due time will follow ; but the present examples will be sufficient to show the object attempted, in the way of scientific instruction, and to impress the mind of the visitor with the importance of the study of natural history, by the means of grouped illustrations.

Crossing the road, and passing the screen, we proceed to examine, on the garden-side of the Palace, the various natural history illustrations of

THE OLD WORLD.

On entering this section of the department will be found two cases of South African birds,—for it is at South Africa we commence our investigation—and immediately before us is seen a group of Zulu Kaffres. This tribe has become especially interesting to Englishmen on account of their long war with the Kaffre people, and of their acquaintance with a number of Zulus who visited this country in 1853. The Kaffre tribes are far above the rest of the South African races : they are in a measure civilized, some of them build houses and towns, and pay considerable attention to arts and manufactures. In general they are tall and well proportioned ; their skin is of a brown colour ; they have woolly hair, high foreheads, and prominent noses, and are of an excessively warlike and predatory disposition. On one side of this group are two Bosjesmen, and on the other two Earthmen, all of whom are generally styled Bushmen ; they fix their abode on unappropriated tracts of land, which frequently separate hostile tribes.

On the right of the visitor, amidst the vegetation of South Africa, are placed a giraffe, a leucoryx, and a bontebok. The giraffe is a male born in London about ten years ago. Its long neck enables it to browse upon the young shoots of tall trees, and to curl around them its tongue, which it can extend a great way, and with which it draws its food into its mouth. As the two-humped camel is peculiarly an Asiatic animal, and the llama a South American one, so is the giraffe peculiar to Africa, and perhaps the most characteristic animal of that rich zoological region.

In the space on the left of the visitor, which is also devoted to South Africa, are groups of a lion and cub, a brown hyæna, and a battle between a leopard and a duyker-bok. Such a

The Giraffe.

battle is not an uncommon occurrence in savage life. The leopard, making too sure of its prey, has fearlessly sprung upon it, and the little antelope has received the attack upon its knees with its head down. No sooner does it feel the claws of its enemy, than it at once partly raises itself, and at the same instant, by means of the great muscular strength which all the deer tribe possess in the head and neck, it buries one of its horns in the ribs of the leopard, whose countenance plainly indicates the deadly nature of the wound. The plants of this region are chiefly heaths. There are also some fine specimens of Polygala and Amphelexis, together with several plants whose aspects are as curious as their names.

Choosing the path to the right, as he faces the group of Kaffres, the visitor will presently arrive at the section which separates Eastern Africa, on the confines of which will be found a female hippopotamus. As this animal is found in both Southern and Eastern Africa, it here occupies an intermediate place between the two provinces. From the fine young male now in the Regent's Park Zoological Gardens, the habits of this animal are too generally known to need comment here. We now come to a group of those Danakils who inhabit the country between Abyssinia and the sea, leading a camel to water. The Danakils are a nomad or wandering tribe; they are of a chocolate-coloured complexion, and have woolly hair, which they dress in a fantastic manner; they are of slender make, tall, and differ widely in appearance from the Negro. The Danakils are transitional between the Negro and the Arab, possess a Jewish physiognomy, and have acquired the Negro element from their intercourse with the neighbouring members of that race. Proceeding a short distance, we find, on the extreme left, a group of slaves, which, with the plants and animals, represent Western Africa. The Negro nations of Guinea are those that have supplied slaves for the Americas. These specimens are typical of the Negroes from the Delta of the Niger, and are chiefly Ibos, but the lighter varieties are the Fellatahs and Nufis, from the interior of the country, and they exhibit less of the Negro type. Near this group will be found three specimens of the chimpanzee, the animal whose form most nearly resembles that of man. It is found only on the Western Coast of Africa, though it may probably also exist in the far interior, where no European as yet has penetrated. Though similar to the ourang outang of Sumatra in general form, the chimpanzee is a smaller animal; it lives in woods, builds huts, uses clubs for attack as well as for defence, and in many ways exhibits an intelligence that presses with rather uncomfortable nearness upon the pride of the sole rational animal.

The Chimpanzee.

Beyond this, and upon the verge of Northern Africa, is represented a battle between two leopards, forcibly reminding us of a quarrel between two cats, which, in fact, it is. Any one who has seen one cat advancing towards another, must have observed that there is always a desire to receive the assault lying on the back, with the four legs upwards. The motive is to be in a position to have free use of the claws of all the legs ; and in the group before us, though the smaller animal appears to have the advantage both by position and by the grip he has taken on the throat of the other, yet the laceration he is receiving underneath from the hind legs of the larger animal, will soon oblige him to release his hold. The vegetation of North Africa includes orange and lemon trees, the date palm, the oleander, the sweet bay tree, and the laurustinus.

On the right we have before us an illustration of Asia, in which the tiger hunt forms a most important feature. The danger of this sport is sufficiently known to all who have engaged in or heard of it. The tiger, seen extended on his back, has been wounded from the howdah, or car on the elephant's back, and in his struggle has rolled over into that position. The other tiger seeks to revenge his companion by an attack upon the persons in the howdah, whilst the elephant is in the act of uttering a roar of fear, and starting off with the speed of terror from the scene of action. Under such circumstances, the keeper, seated on the neck of the animal, has no control over him, and the riders are in imminent peril of being jolted out of their seats, and of falling into the clutches of the tiger. Near this episode of hunting-life in India will be found a group of Hindoos, in which will be readily distinguished two distinct kinds of physiognomy, one coarse-featured and dark-skinned—the low caste—and the other with fine features, and lighter-skinned—the high caste. The Hindoos belong to the Indo-European nations, and are spread over British India ; some of them are exceedingly handsome, possessing small foreheads and black lively eyes ; they are physically weak, and incapable of hard, manual labour. Some are very skilful artisans, and employ their time in painting on ivory, in wood-carving, and in manufacturing the beautiful Indian shawls and fine cloths so much esteemed by Europeans. The most conspicuous shrubs here are the Indian Rhododendrons, contrasting with the American Rhododendrons in the New World. Here are also the India-rubber tree, the Assam tea plant, and the drooping Juniperus recurva. Opposite the group of Hindoos the visitor will see a lion and lioness with a cub under the shade of some orange trees, as further illustrations of North Africa. Near them is a specimen of the Barbary Ape, the only monkey found in Europe. He is seen in the wild state inhabiting the caverns of impregnable Gibraltar.

Further on, and on the left of the visitor, will be seen a group representing the population of Chinese Tartary, and several specimens of Asiatic animals, including the large-horned sheep called Ovis Ammon, which is exceedingly rare ; the Yaks, or grunting oxen, which are used by the Tartars for riding or driving, as well as for food or clothing ; the tail being very much in request

The Yak.

in India for brushing away flies, no less than as an emblem of authority ; and the Ounce, an animal which three hundred years ago was comparatively well known, but whose skin has since become so rare that the very existence of the animal has been questioned.

I

European travellers have lately visited its haunts in Central Asia, and satisfactorily proved that it still lives. The most conspicuous plants are the Camellias and the Indian arbor vitæ, which is the Asiatic representative of the similar plant in the new world. Amongst this botanical group will be found also specimens of the black and green tea plants.

Let the visitor now pass under the staircases leading to the galleries, and, bearing somewhat to the right, he will come to a small plot of ground dedicated to the illustration of Australia and New Guinea. Selecting the left-hand path, he will first notice a case of marine objects, consisting of the mollusques, corals, &c., of Australia, and advancing a few paces, will find, on his left, a small piece of ground devoted to New Guinea. The ethnological group are the Papuans of New Guinea, easily distinguishable by their curious, frizzled hair, which makes their heads resemble mops; they are neither Malays, nor Negroes, but a mixed race between the two, retaining the characteristics of the tribes from which they sprung : hence they may be called Malay-Negroes. Turning to the right from this group, a few steps conduct us to a case filled with Australian birds, and then proceeding towards the entrance to this portion of our geographical illustrations, we have on our right a general illustration of Australia ; and on the left another marine case. Amongst the animals will be noticed that most characteristic form, the kangaroo. The Australian men here depicted strike us at once by their half-starved, lanky, and ill-proportioned bodies ; they may be looked upon as savages, hunters, and inhabitants of forests ; they possess that excessive projection of the jaw which ethnologists make one of the distinguishing traits in the most degraded forms of man.

Here the visitor will find numerous plants with which he is acquainted in conservatories ; the Banksia, the Acacias, and the different kinds of Epacris and Eriostemon, are amongst the most conspicuous. He will see also specimens of three other kinds of Araucaria, the most elegant of which is the Norfolk Island Pine.

Quitting this part, and proceeding up the building in a northerly direction, after crossing the transept we find, close to the open, corridor looking out on the gardens, a plot of ground devoted to the illustration of the Indian isles. The principal group of men represents a party of the natives of Borneo in their war dresses, and to the left is a group of Sumatrans, with three opium eaters from Java ; there will likewise be noticed a black leopard and two Malay bears.

The plants of the Indian islands, with the exception of those beautiful Orchids (for the growth of which our building is not sufficiently warm or humid), are not to be procured in England. The vegetation of these regions is, accordingly, unrepresented. Our illustrations here are conventional and picturesque.

With this group we complete our rapid survey of the Natural History department of the Crystal Palace. It remains to mention that the Ethnological section has been formed under the direction of Dr. Latham; that the Zoological Collection has been formed by Mr. G. R. Waterhouse; that Mr. Gould has formed the Ornithological Collection, and that Sir Joseph Paxton has selected the plants to illustrate the Botany. The whole of the Natural History arrangements have been effected under the general direction of Professor Edward Forbes, and the personal superintendence of Mr. Wm. Thomson.

Turning now to the left, a few paces bring us to the side of the first Industrial Court; or, of

THE MUSICAL INSTRUMENT COURT.

This Court displays much inventive fancy in its general design and execution, and may fairly challenge comparison with any architectural novelty in the Palace. It is the production of Mr. John Thomas, who is well known as the sculptor of the statues at the new Houses of Parliament. The aim of the architect here has been, not so much to build a mere Court for the exhibition of musical instruments, as to produce a Temple dedicated to Music, and to render the architectural detail and ornament typical of the high and beautiful art as well as of the subservient mechanical craft. The end of the Court before which we are now standing is symbolical of Sacred Music. Over the two doorways are alto-relievo figures of Miriam and David, and in the centre is a bust of Jubal. The three-quarter columns are of a composite design, part of the shaft being made to represent organ-pipes. Turning into the nave, we advance towards the principal side, or rather front of the Court, which is divided into three compartments, and may be regarded as the typification of mythological and primitive music, a head of Apollo appearing in the centre, the frieze along the whole length of this side being ornamented with heads of Pan, lyres, sea-shells, and other instruments of sound. In front are the statues of Musidora to the left and Diana to the right; the recumbent figures near them are allegorical of Night (to the left) and Morning. Entering

through one of the central openings, we find the interior of the
Court more highly decorated than the exterior. Over the
entrances are figures of St. Cecilia and Erato, under which are
lines from Dryden and Collins. Round the other portions of
the Court are ranged the busts of the most celebrated English
and foreign composers, and on the frieze are figures of boys
playing upon various instruments. In fact the whole Court,
externally and internally, is descriptive of the music of all ages and
all countries; whilst the pleasant subdued colouring harmonizes
charmingly with the pervading spirit. Making his way round this
court by the usual route, viz., from right to left, the visitor will
notice the places appropriated to pianofortes, harps, drums, wind
and stringed instruments. The windows of this court afford a
favourable opportunity for exhibiting printed music. On issuing
into the nave we come next to the

PRINTED FABRICS COURT.

This court represents a branch of trade peculiarly belonging to
England, and one indeed, in which, until of late, she has been
almost without a competitor; viz., the manufacture and printing
of cotton and woollen goods. The architects, Messrs. Banks and
Barry, have adorned the walls of this court with medallion portraits
of the eminent men to whose genius we are indebted for improvements in this particular branch of manufacture; and the frieze, with
bas-reliefs representing the introduction of the raw material into
this country, and the several processes through which the same
material passes, until it finally quits England again in its most
highly finished and useful form. No particular style is followed
in this court: the architects have suited their fancy by appro-
priating what they found picturesque in several styles; and the
character of the court may be called decorative Italian, combined
with Elizabethan, and even Byzantine features. Entering through
the central opening, the most important object in the interior is an
allegorical figure of Manchester placed in the centre: a distinction
due to the city which is the heart of the cotton trade of the
country. Next in order to this court we reach the

MIXED FABRICS COURT.

This Court has been erected by Professor Gottfried Semper. It is divided into two parts : one covered by a ceiling, for the reception of the more delicate fabrics likely to suffer by exposure to the sun's rays, and which may be seen to better advantage in a subdued light ; and the other uncovered, and appropriated to raw produce, and such textile manufactures as are not susceptible of injury from sunshine. The style of decoration employed is *Cinque Cento*, and the ornaments are, as in other cases, symbolical of the manufactures to which the Court is dedicated.

On the tympanum above the entrance to the covered portion is placed a head of Minerva, the traditional inventress of spinning and weaving. In the panels on either side of the head will be paintings of the olive tree, sacred to Minerva, and, in our idea, to Peace, the true protecting goddess of human industry. On the roof of the covered portion will be placed a fountain, composed of Majolica ware, at the angles of which are placed small figures of boys on sheep, and the general decorations of which are symbolical of weaving and spinning. This fountain will, however, be better seen from the gallery above.

Entering through the opening in the semicircular uncovered portion, on either side of which are pedestals, to be surmounted by typical groups, we may first examine the decorations of the Court, and then the contents of the glass cases, which include hosiery, shawls, and other textile fabrics. After this we enter the covered division. The lower portion of the Court is occupied with glass cases, and above are placed ornamental columns, supporting the ceiling ; the latter is panelled in oak, and the insides of the panels are filled in with representations of the hemp and flax plants, from which linen is manufactured ; mulberry bushes, the leaves of which are the food of the silk-worm ; and the symbolical Golden Fleece, all painted on blue and red grounds. On the ceiling also are tablets inscribed with the names of the principal continental and English manufacturing towns. In this court are exhibited manufactured silks, India and China shawls, and other costly and delicate fabrics.

Quitting this collection of manufacture, we pass on, in the nave, to the

FOREIGN INDUSTRIAL COURT.

Conspicuous amidst the articles of art and manufacture exhibited in this Court are the specimens of Sévres porcelain and Gobelin tapestry, sent for exhibition at the Crystal Palace from the Imperial manufactories of France by his Majesty the Emperor of the French. The Gobelins factory at Paris is celebrated for its tapestry work and carpets ; and the quarter of the city in which it is situated has for four or five centuries past been inhabited by wool-dyers, for the sake of a valuable and peculiar stream of water that passes through it. Jean Gobelin, a wool-dyer, lived here in the 15th century, and amassed a large fortune in his trade, which after his death was carried on for a time by his descendants, who having in their turn become rich, allowed the business to pass into other hands. Their successors, the Messrs. Canaye, added a new branch of trade—the manufacture of tapestry, which until then had been confined to Flanders. Louis XIV. purchased the factory from these proprietors ; and the Gobelins, which has since remained crown property, was in 1826 made also the seat of the royal manufactory of carpets. Le Brun, the painter, was appointed director of the Gobelins in 1667, and painted his "Battles of Alexander the Great" as patterns for tapestry. At the present time many eminent artists and chemists are connected with the factory, including M. Chevreuil, whose connexion with the Gobelins has led to the production of a most valuable and complete work on the contrasts of colour.

The manufactory of Sévres porcelain was originally established at Vincennes ; but in the middle of the last century the farmers-general purchased and transferred it to the little village of Sévres, situated a few miles from Paris. Louis XV., in compliance with the wish of Madame de Pompadour, afterwards bought it from the farmers-general, and, like the Gobelins manufactory, this, too, has since remained the property of the crown.

Porcelain is of two kinds, soft and hard, and up to 1770, the former only was produced in France ; but after that period the latter also was manufactured at Sévres. Common earthenware vessels are soft : white stone ware and crockery are hard : and hard porcelain during the last century was alone considered worthy of the name, the manufacture being confined chiefly to China and Japan. In 1761, however, the secret of its composition had been imparted to the director of the Sévres works, who was, however, unable to produce the superior ware in consequence of the scarcity of the white *Kaolin*, or clay, employed in its production. A large quantity of this material having been shortly afterwards accidentally discovered at Limoges, in France, the manufacture of hard porcelain of the finest quality was commenced, and has ever since been carried on, at Sévres. The common specimens of Sévres china are ornamented with beautifully painted flowers on a plain ground; but the more splendid pieces have grounds of various colours, including those most highly prized and beautiful, the Rose Dubarry and the Bleu de Roi. When the first named ground is employed the cups are frequently jewelled, and generally these splendid examples are decorated with the most beautiful paintings of fruits, flowers, and figures. The specimens painted with subjects after Watteau are much prized.

Specimens of Sévres china command large sums amongst collectors, and like most objects of *vertu* are often fraudulently imitated. Attached to the Sévres factory is a museum, in which are placed specimens of all the different kinds of china manufactured there since its establishment, and a most valuable collection of works in ceramic ware of all ages and nations. We may add, that this manufactory, in the hands of government, is not a profitable speculation, and barely covers its necessary expenses.

This Court was originally entrusted to a French architect, who, late in the spring, on account of the short period allowed for its construction, declined its execution. At the eleventh hour, Sir Joseph Paxton took it in hand, and in the short space of one month the Court has risen from its foundations to its present state of completeness, the builder being Mr. George Myers. The style chosen by Sir Joseph Paxton is late Gothic. It is built, like the Stationery Court, chiefly of wood, the construction not being concealed, but allowed to appear, and emblazoned with colour. The lower panels facing the nave are of silvered-plate glass, and above are panels ornamented with beautiful examples of illuminated art. The decorations of the interior consist of shields emblazoned with the arms of various nations, and legendary scrolls setting forth the names of the principal seats of manufacture.

This Court concludes the series of Industrial establishments erected within the Crystal Palace for the display of the skill of England and of other nations. The attempt to collect under one roof the best specimens of various trades whose seats of manufacture are scattered over the world, is now for the first time made in connexion with the most elevating exhibition ever offered for the instruction and enlightenment of man. The union of industry and Fine Art first formed in the Crystal Palace of 1851, but severed at the close of a few months, is here permanently consolidated and secured. The advantages to both purchaser and seller offered by this gigantic museum of intellectual and manual production are self-evident. Here the manufacturer and trades-man may bring his specimen, assured of an admirable site for exposition : and here the purchaser has an opportunity of com-paring the best works of different hands, and lands, without the labour and fatigue of journeying from shop to shop in search of his requirements. His selections made—a school of art, unrivalled in the world, solicits his contemplation, and a garden, of beauty certainly unmatched in England, invites to repose and restoration.

Quitting the last Industrial Court, and turning to the right towards the garden, we reach the Photographic Departmemt entrusted to Mr. P. H. Delamotte, the photographer to the Crystal Palace Company, for the exhibition of the views of the Palace and grounds—illustrations, of a kind promising to displace the unsatis-factory prints which of late years have formed the sole questionable ornament for the walls of the working classes.

The visitor having explored all the Fine Art Courts as well as the several Courts of Manufacture, may now give his exclusive attention to the *chef-d'œuvres* and valuable examples of ancient and modern sculpture, which he has not found -in the Fine Art Courts ; but which will arrest his eye from point to point, as he accompanies us in

A WALK THROUGH THE NAVE.

Our starting point shall be the screen of the kings and queens of England, at the south end of the building, containing casts of the regal statues at the new Houses of Parliament, Westminster, executed by Mr. John Thomas.

The screen itself is from the design of Mr. M. D. Wyatt, and is characterized by much originality and appropriateness of treat-ment. The series of monarchs is placed in chronological order, commencing, on the return side to the left (as we face the screen), with the kings of the Saxon heptarchy ; and beneath them the Saxon kings, the first on the left being Egbert, by whom the greater number of the petty kingdoms were first consolidated. The Norman series commences, on the principal front, with

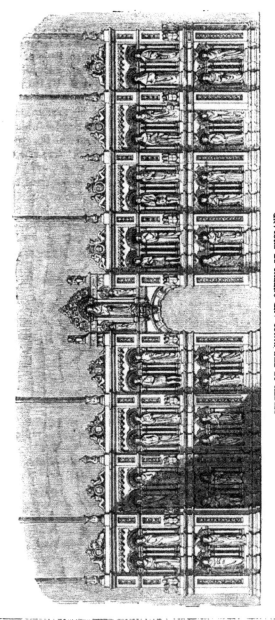

SCREEN OF THE KINGS AND QUEENS OF ENGLAND.

William I. and his queen, above whom are the statues of St. George and St. Andrew. Amongst the various rulers of the state may be noticed as of great excellence, in that style of sculpture which has been termed "the Romantic," Henry II., Berengaria, Henry V., Henry VI., Richard III., Edward VI., Charles the First and his Queen Henrietta, and Cromwell; this last was rejected by the Committee of the Houses of Parliament, but is clearly necessary for completing the historical series which is concluded on the return side, to the right, with the royal personages of the reigning Guelph family, and a lower row of Saxon kings.

Quitting the screen, we are first attracted on our road by Osler's Crystal Fountain, which occupied so conspicuous a place in the Great Exhibition in Hyde Park. On the water which surrounds it, float the gigantic leaves of the Victoria Regia, the Nymphæa Nelumbia, and other tropical plants. We will now proceed to the west end of the south, or Norwood transept, in which is placed a cast of the well-known

EQUESTRIAN STATUE OF CHARLES I.

from the original at Charing Cross. It was designed and executed in 1633, by Hubert Le Sueur, a French sculptor, pupil of the celebrated John of Bologna, but was not at the time raised on its intended site. During the civil wars, the Parliament, wanting men more than statues, sold it to John Rivet, a brazier, living in Holborn; by him it was kept concealed until the restoration of Charles II., when it returned again into the hands of the government, and was finally erected at Charing Cross in 1674. The pedestal is a work of the celebrated sculptor Grinling Gibbons.

Beyond the statue of Charles I. in the central line, is placed that of James II. by Grinling Gibbons, cast from the original now in the court at the back of Whitehall. It is an excellent example of a portrait statue treated in the classical style; and affords us a proof of the higher reach of Gibbons's genius; whose well-earned reputation in the seventeenth century, we may remark, rested more especially on his works in ornamental carving, of which the exquisitely cut fruits, flowers, wreaths and other ornaments on the façade of St. Paul's, London, are examples.

A selection from the best productions of various English sculptors surrounds this portion of the transept. At the south angle is the original model of the colossal statue of the great Earl of Chatham (449),* forming a portion of his monument in Westminster Abbey. It was executed by J. Bacon, R.A., a contemporary sculptor, who was celebrated for the truth and vigour of his portraits. Bacon should also be mentioned with honour, as one of the first native artists who founded the English school of sculpture in the last half of the eighteenth century. Amongst the statues in the transept itself, we would notice Macdonald's excellent compositions of Ulysses recognised by his Dog (48), and Andromeda (45) ; the very gracefully designed figure of a Bather (36), by Lawlor, and a group of Boys Contending for a Prize, by the same artist. Near the entrance are placed two figures of Dogs, cast from the antique, and the well-known Florentine Boar : the originals of these are in the gallery at Florence.

The statues on the north side of this end of the transept are principally by Spence and Theed, amongst them will be remarked the Highland Mary (58), and the statue of Flora (59), both by Spence ; Narcissus at the Fountain (60), and Psyche (61), by Theed.

At the junction of the Transept and the Nave is placed the colossal statue of Dr. Johnson, from his monument at St. Paul's, the first that was erected in that Cathedral. This portrait-statue, as that of Chatham, is by Bacon ; but composed, as will be remarked, on a diametrically opposite principle ; the great writer being half clad in a classic toga, whilst the great statesman, is brought more vividly to our minds by being represented in the costume of his period and his order.

Proceeding in front of the Pompeian Court on this side of the Nave, will be found various works illustrative of modern German sculpture ; amongst which we notice a prettily conceived figure of a Child-Christ (163), designed for the Royal Christmas tree, by Blaeser of Berlin, and a group of Minerva Protecting a Warrior (162), by the same sculptor.

A charming little composition, by Brugger, of a "Centaur" instructing the young Achilles (No. 164). The original model of a nymph, with an urn (167), by Dannecker, executed as a fountain at Stuttgard. An allegorical figure of Medicine (171), by Hahnel of Dresden. Two seated statues, in the Greek style, of Thucydides and Homer (176), by Launitz. A statue of a Magdalen (261), by Wagner. A statue of Hector (166), by

* This number refers to "The Handbook to the Portrait Gallery."

Dannecker.   A very spirited group of a Hunter defending his
family against a Panther (264), by Widermann, of Munich * ;
the statue of a Hunter (263), is a *chef-d'œuvre* by Wittig.
Opposite the Stationery Court are excellent life-size statues of
stags (193*), by Professor Rauch, of Berlin, excellent examples of
that difficult branch of the sculptor's art—the study of animal
nature.   Beyond the Stationery Court, a little to the back, is a
very beautiful group of a Pietà (196*), by Rietschel, of Dresden.
The fine statues of Victory (184 to 188 inclusive), by Professor
Rauch, are characteristic examples of that great sculptor's style,
and of the successful variety of treatment in five designs for one
and the same subject.   And the statue of a Nymph holding a
Basket of Fruits and Flowers (160), by Professor Drake, is a
picturesque example of the "Romantic" school.   A little beyond
this is the Court of

ENGLISH AND GERMAN SCULPTURE,

which we may enter and explore with advantage.

In this Court is placed a selection of the finest productions of
the English and German schools of modern sculpture, prominent
amongst which is seen the noble colossal head of Bavaria, by
Ludwig Schwanthaler, of Munich, who enjoyed a European celebrity.
The original bronze statue to which it belongs, erected outside the
city of Munich, is fifty feet in height, the pedestal on which it
stands being thirty feet high.   For ten years did the great
artist, weak and broken in health, still devote himself with a true
artist's love to the progress of his task : but he was not destined
to witness its perfect completion ; and when the statue of the
Genius of Bavaria was cast in bronze, its author had passed from
amongst us.   The statue was first publicly exhibited in 1850.

Opposite the head of Bavaria, is another example of those
embodiments of towns and nations, which are so frequently to be
found on the Continent.   The present colossal statue allegorizes
Franconia, a province of Germany ; it is characterized by much
nobility of conception, and worthily sustains the reputation of the
modern German sculptors.   The original, by Professor Halbig, is
erected at Kilheim, in Bavaria.

In the centre stands a part of the monument of Frederick the
Great at Berlin, designed by Professor Rauch ; and near to it is

---

* These numbers refer to those in the "Handbook of Modern Sculpture."

placed a small model, showing the complete monument. The equestrian statue of the King, which surmounts the largest of the two, deserves particular attention, as one of the finest examples of modern portrait sculpture ; whilst the artistic management of the costume, the drapery of the cloak, and the general success seen in the treatment of modern costume, constitute the statue, in this respect, also, a model in art.

Amongst other works representative of the German school, may be noticed two statues of Nymphs by Schwanthaler (Nos. 202 and 203), remarkable for their beauty of form. Placed on either side of the head of Bavaria, are two colossal "Victories," by the same artist, from the "Ruhmeshalle," or Hall of Fame, at Munich. The life-size statue of a Danaid (188), by Rauch, also deserves especial notice, whilst Tieck's charming collection of statuettes (Nos. 253, 254, 255, 256, 257, and 258) claims equal praise.

Several examples of the works of the celebrated Thorwaldsen will also be found collected in this Court, and evoke especial admiration for the beauty of their forms, for their ideality of expression, and for the purity of sentiment which characterizes their conception. Amongst them we would particularly point out "Venus with the Apple" (217), the Three Graces (222), Mercury (219), and the very beautiful bas-reliefs on the wall, illustrating the triumphs of Alexander (226).

Amongst the productions of the English school, we would draw attention to Crawford's graceful statue of Flora (10), Wyatt's Bather (77), and a Nymph with an Urn (76).

On quitting this Court (towards the great transept) we enter that section of

THE PORTRAIT GALLERY

which is devoted to the portrait-busts of celebrated Germans ; amongst them will be found the greatest names from that crowd of remarkable men, of whom Germany, in modern times, has been the prolific mother. They are arranged chronologically and in regular succession as artists, musicians, poets, dramatists, scientific men, authors, statesmen, soldiers, prelates, theologians, and royal personages ; amongst them are to be remarked Beethoven (321), Mendelssohn (331), Goethe (337), Blucher (360), Berzelius (354), Handel (314 A), Humboldt (351), Radetzky (370), and the reigning King of Prussia (384).* In order the better to appreciate this,

* These numbers refer to those marked in "Handbook to the Portrait Gallery."

and the three remaining sections of the Portrait Gallery, we refer the visitor to the Handbook of the Portrait Gallery, which contains not only a notice of the lives, but general information as to the character and claims to renown, of the several notabilities.

Returning to the nave, the visitor will find, at the angle of the great transept, a cast from the colossal bronze statue of Sir Robert Peel by Marochetti, from Manchester ; and turning at this point, to the left, may proceed to examine the statues and monuments at the west end of the great transept. The subjects ranged in front of the German portrait gallery, are selections from the works of the Roman school of English sculpture, including a fine collection of the works of Gibson and Wyatt. Amongst the principal productions of the latter, may be noticed Penelope (82),* a charming group of Ino and Bacchus (73), Zephyr and Flora (80), a Huntress (79), and a graceful composition of a Girl with a Lamb (81). The chief works of Gibson's chisel are the Flora (14) ; a very beautifully conceived Venus (13) ; the wounded Amazon (16), which it will be interesting to compare with the same subject, the work of an ancient Greek sculptor (to be noticed shortly) ; a Hunter holding in a Dog (20) ; the graceful statue of Hylas (22) ; Cupid disguised as a Shepherd (15), and the very elegant group of Aurora borne by the Zephyrs (21).

The central place, at this end of the great transept, is occupied by

THE CHORAGIC MONUMENT OF LYSICRATES.

This beautiful example of ancient Greek architecture is usually styled the Lantern of Demosthenes, on account of a tradition, which ascribes its erection to that celebrated orator. No weight, however, can be attached to this supposition, although it may be, and in all probability is, due to the time of Demosthenes.

An inscription on the architrave informs us that this monument was erected by Lysicrates of Kikyna, at his own expense, in order to commemorate a musical triumph obtained by various members of his tribe or clan, the Akamantis. The ancient Greeks were in the habit of holding a species of musical tournament, in which the most celebrated masters of the art vied with each other; in this particular case, the palm was awarded to Theon, the flute-

* These numbers refer to those in the " Handbook of Modern Sculpture."

player, and the chorus of boys led by Lysiades ; the magistrate for the year being Evanectus. It was to celebrate this triumph that the monument was erected ; the tripod at the summit being the prize awarded, and on it was sculptured the story of Bacchus transforming the Tyrrhenian pirates into dolphins, which was the subject of the music. A tripod was the usual prize granted in these contests, and the victor either placed it in one of the temples, or, as in the present instance, consecrated a monument specially for its reception.

Around the pedestal of this interesting work are placed four noble Greek statues of Zeno (321), Aristides (322), Æschines (323), and Phocion (324), and on either side are seen the celebrated statues of men and horses, now at Rome, on the Quirinal hill, generally known as

THE MONTE CAVALLO GROUP.

The figures are supposed to represent Castor and Pollux, and the two groups are respectively attributed to the sculptors Phidias and Praxiteles, their names being found engraved on them. They are admirable and striking works, remarkable for the life and vigorous action displayed in them.

Passing these ancient classic monuments, and directing our steps along the northern side of the transept, we find several works of Greek sculpture, including a poetically conceived statue of Polyhymnia (341). The spirited figure of the Dancing Faun (352), from Florence. The admirable seated portrait statue of Posidònius (342). The Sleeping Faun (408). A copy of Venus de' Medici. A statue of Mercury, seated. The Discobolus of Nausidas, from Naples. And the wounded Amazon (330). Amongst the remaining subjects, the Faun with a Goat may be selected as a characteristic example of the Roman style of sculpture.

At the back of these, will be found another section of the Portrait gallery, consisting of the busts of celebrated Englishmen and Americans, arranged as previously described in the German portrait section ; among the most remarkable may be selected— Inigo Jones * (388), Sir C. Wren (389), Garrick (390), Flaxman (394), Bacon (420), Locke (422), Newton (423), Franklin (424 A), Adam Smith (426), and Washington (451).

* These numbers refer to those marked in the Handbook to "Portrait Gallery."

At the junction of this angle of the great transept with the nave,
is placed the celebrated Farnese Hercules, from the Museum at
Naples; a fine example of antique sculpture, characterized by a
massive and somewhat exaggerated muscular development, not
however altogether inappropriate to the Hero of Physical force.
Keeping still to the left, along the nave, we remark several
antique statues including the Antinous as Mercury from the
Capitol at Rome (316), and the Adonis from Capua (213).

Before reaching the Egyptian Court, we turn to the left, and a
few steps bring us to the

GREEK AND ROMAN SCULPTURE COURT,

In which, as the name denotes, are collected some of the *chef-
d'œuvres* of the Greek and Roman schools; the first group that
attracts the eye, being that in the centre of the Court, known as
the

TORO FARNESE, OR FARNESE BULL.

The original of this beautiful group, which is now preserved in
the Museum at Naples, was discovered in the Baths of Caracalla
at Rome, and derives its name from having been placed in the
Farnese Palace in that city.   The subject is the revenge of Queen
Antiope and her two sons, Zethus and Amphion, on Dirce, for
seducing the affections of her husband, Syeres, King of Thebes.
The sons, enraged at the insult offered to their mother, are represented as about to revenge themselves by tying the unfortunate
Dirce to the horns of a bull, when their mother, moved with
womanly pity, intercedes for her rival, and induces them to forego
the intended punishment.   According to Pliny, the Toro Farnese
was the work of the Rhodian artists, Apollonius and Tauriseus.
Among other remarkable subjects in this Court, we would draw
attention to the colossal "Velletri Pallas," (407) so called from
having been discovered at Velletri, near Rome, and now preserved
in the Louvre, at Paris; the Dying Gladiator (309); a Boy with
a Dolphin; and a colossal head of Pallas (409).

A fine collection of Greek ideal and portrait busts will also be
noticed in this Court; amongst which the colossal heads of Vespasian (332),* Trajan (354), Pertinax (379), Lucius Verus (361),
and Titus (333), are particularly deserving of notice.   The visitor

---

* These numbers refer to those in the "Handbook to the Greek Court and
Nave."

should not quit this compartment without noticing the collection of antique vases which it contains, amongst which the Medicean Vase (343) is a peculiarly elegant example of antique art.

Retracing our steps, we once more regain the Nave, and advancing in front of the Egyptian Court, remark several works of Greek art, including a statue of Bacchus (311).

From this point, extending throughout the façade of the Greek Court, are ranged excellent examples of Greek sculpture, which the visitor may compare with the subsequent works of the Roman sculptors, or of Greeks settled at Rome, placed before the walls of the Roman Court. Amongst the Greek statues we select the group of Silenus and a youthful Bacchus (306), excellently treated and full of life; [seated statues of Demosthenes the philosopher (303); and of Posidonius (307), on each side of the first entrance to the Court; a Bacchus and Faun (305); the fine group of the Wrestlers, from Florence (304), the well-known Drunken Faun (295), from the Museum at Naples; and the Apollo Sauroctonus (298), from the Vatican.* Nor must we omit the excellent seated statues (271, 290).

In front of the Roman Court will be first noticed Meleager and his dog (289); the fine Mercury from the Vatican (287), and the same subject (288) from Naples. Before the first entrance to the court are placed the seated statues of Trajan and Agrippina.

The Mercury disguised as a shepherd (285), and the Adonis (282),† are characteristic specimens of the ordinary Roman style.

Passing the façade of the Alhambra Court, we arrive at the Fountains, which at this end of the Nave correspond to those of the south end, in position, and with respect to the aquatic plants which live in the water of the long basin. The two fountains here are designed by Monti the sculptor. The figures of Syrens, supporting the large shells, typify by their colour four races of men: the Caucasian, white; the Nubian, black; the North American Indian, red; and the Australian, olive. The smaller figures above these bear fruit indigenous to various soils. The design of the Fountains is most appropriate, and the entire composition very artistic. The bronze colour of these statues and of many others, in the building, is produced by means of the electrotype process with signal success.

Traversing the Avenue of Sphinxes—to be noticed on our return-

---

* These numbers refer to those in "Handbook in Greek Court."
† These and the following numbers refer to those in "Handbook to Roman Court and Nave."

down the garden side, from which point a better view of the whole
transept is gained—we pass a variety of Palms, Bananas, and
other tropical plants, continued throughout this part of the nave,
and rendered. more agreeable to the eye by the addition of an
artificial soil and rock-work.

Beyond this portion, and at the extreme north end of the nave,
are placed

THE ÆGINA MARBLES.

These most interesting monuments of ancient Greek art are now
in the Glyptothek at Munich.

They were discovered in the island of Ægina, and are supposed
to have ornamented the tympana of the east and west fronts of
the temple of Minerva in that island.   The group, representing the
contest over the body of Patroclus, belonged to the western ; and
the five figures descriptive of the battle of Hercules and Telamon
against the Trojan king Laomedon were in the eastern tympanum.
They are most remarkable examples of Greek sculpture during its
second period, or from the close of the sixth to the middle of the
fifth century B. C.

The conception, the anatomy, and beauty of form found in
these statues denote a highly cultivated artistic taste and power,
to which the peculiar faces, the invariable smile on the mouth, and
a certain stiff angularity of treatment, form a marked contrast.
We observe in them that turning-point in the history of Greek
sculpture, when the conventionalities of an earlier system were
receding before that love of nature and extraordinary perception of
the beautiful, which subsequently rendered the Greeks so pre-
eminent in art.

The originals, which had, as may be supposed, suffered considerably from the effects of time, were restored by Thorwaldsen,
the Dane, whose conscientious spirit and thorough appreciation of
the antique give assurance of the correctness of the interesting
exa   now before us.

     ncing our return journey down the garden side of the
     turn our steps towards the artificial rock-work, covered
     al foliage, and arrive at a fountain of toilet vinegar,
     Mr. E. Rimmel, from a design by Mr. John Thomas, by
     our statues placed at the angles of the fountain are also
     Continuing onwards, we obtain a fine view of the north
     th its noble avenue of sphinxes and palm trees, termi-

THE TEMPLE OF ABOO SIMBEL.

THE COLOSSAL EGYPTIAN FIGURES,

which are from the temple of Rameses the Great at Aboo Simbel, in Nubia. These immense seated statues towering to the roof of the transept afford us some adequate idea of the stupendous magnitude and passive grandeur which characterize the monuments of ancient Egyptian art. Their height is 65 feet.

It may be remembered that in the Egyptian Court we directed the attention of the visitor to a model of the temple at Aboo Simbel; on the façade of which were four statues of Rameses the Great. Two of these statues are here reproduced on the scale of the originals, the smaller figures around them representing the mother, wife, and daughter of the king.

The temple of Aboo Simbel, in Nubia, is excavated from the rock, and was first discovered by Burckhardt, the traveller; the accumulated sand of centuries, which then covered it, was removed by order of Belzoni, the first, with Captains Irby and Mangles, to pass its long closed entrance. The interior was covered with paintings and hieroglyphics relating to Rameses the Great, and the date of the temple has been consequently placed at about 1560 B.C.

The sphinxes which formed the avenue are cast from one preserved in the Louvre, the writing engraved on which presents us with a curious but not uncommon instance of a custom that prevailed amongst the Egyptian monarchs. On one side of the shoulder the name "Pthalomen Miotph" is written in hieroglyphics, and on the other shoulder is the name of Shishak I. The last named lived about 1000 B.C., and the first nearly two hundred years before him. Other instances occur where the name of the original founder has been erased altogether, in order to make way for the name of some comparatively modern king.

Leaving the fountain on our right, we arrive almost immediately in front of the Byzantine Court, where, resting beneath the foliage, are six effigies of knights from the Temple Church, London. They are clad, with one exception, in ring-mail, and afford us perfect representations of military costume in the early part of the 13th century. They are usually called the Knights Templar; but without evidence: the cross-legged statues are probably crusaders. The entire series have been carefully restored by Mr. Richardson. The two first statues in front of the German Mediæval Court, as we face the entrance, are fine examples of German Gothic sculpture, from Cologne and Nuremberg: the three subjects beyond them are from Langen

Church, Germany. The two first statues on our right are from the façade of Wells Cathedral, and next to them are various examples of German sculpture. Facing the English Mediæval Court, will be noticed, on each side of the entrance, the effigies of Bishop Kilkenny from Ely Cathedral, Henry III. from Westminster, and of Longespée from Salisbury Cathedral: the two last being especially interesting monuments of the 13th century.

On the right of the entrance, and nearest to the nave, are two statues from Wells Cathedral, noticeable as fine examples of Early English sculpture, and the effigy of Bishop Northwold from Ely. Nearer the façade is placed the remarkable effigy of Queen Philippa, the wife of Edward III., from Westminster Abbey, belonging to the last half of the 14th century. Beyond this again, will be noticed the effigy from Salisbury Cathedral, of Bishop Poer, who died in 1228, one of the earliest monumental statues in England. In front of the façade of the French Mediæval Court, will be found several pieces of Gothic sculpture of the early period of the Pointed style, from Chartres Cathedral; on the right of the entrance from the nave are placed the busts of Henry II. and Diana of Poictiers, Bayard and Louis XII., and nearer to the nave will be seen the Virgin " de Trumeau," from Notre Dame, at Paris; and a fine picturesque bronze statue of a knight from the monument of Maximilian, of Innspruck, in the Austrian Tyrol, a remarkable work of art, executed by native artists in the early part of the 16th century. Further on is placed the fine bronze statue of Albert of Bavaria, from the tomb of Lewis of Bavaria, at Munich, remarkable as serving to illustrate the very rich and characteristic costume of the close of the 16th century. Opposite to it is the very fine St. George, by Donatello, from Florence, one of the masterpieces of that celebrated sculptor, whilst another Innspruck statue occupies a position nearer the nave. Advancing onwards, still in front of the Renaissance Court, we recognise amongst the busts, those of Francis I., Sully and Henry IV. of France, Shakspeare, Machiavelli, Ben Jonson, Cosmo de' Medici, and Lord Bacon. The statues on each side of the path are from the Tartarughe fountain, at Rome, the extreme figure being the celebrated Bacchus, by Michael Angelo. Amongst the works of Italian art placed in front of the Italian Court, we remark the Bacchus by Sansovino, from Florence, the Triton from the gardens of the Doria palace, Genoa, the Tartarughe statues from Rome, and at the angle, in front of the Italian vestibule, the beautiful statue of Mercury, by John of

Bologna, a *chef-d'œuvre* of the 16th century school. Among the busts will be remarked those of Raffaelle and Michael Angelo, Inigo Jones and other celebrities of the Renaissance period.

Still advancing, a few steps to the left, will lead us into

THE GOTHIC RENAISSANCE SCULPTURE COURT

Or "Court of Monuments of Christian Art."

The first subjects that attract our notice as we enter are the very interesting crosses of the early Irish Church, and the richly sculptured bronze column from Hildesheim Cathedral in Germany, a fine example of the Byzantine period.

Beyond these are monuments of the Gothic period, amongst which are conspicuous the Cantilupe shrine from Hereford Cathedral, and the effigy of Edward III., from Westminster. The central tombs of Bishop Wakeman, from Tewkesbury, and of Bishop Bridport, from Salisbury (the last-named being that to the left).

The tomb of Henry VII., an interesting example of the Italian Renaissance style in England, at an early period of its introduction, and the fine monument of Cardinal Zeno from Venice, occupy the further end; and the equestrian statue of Gattamelata, by Donatello, forms a conspicuous feature in this portion of the Court, which is completed with a cast of the celebrated Moses, by Michael Angelo.

As we quit this Court, we remark in front of it two statues of Perseus : one by Cellini, and the other by Canova. That on the left, as we face the Court, by Cellini, is characterized by a grandeur of conception and power of execution, which place his name among those of the greatest sculptors of his day.

For minute and interesting information respecting the monuments, and all the statues on this side of the Palace, the visitor is referred to the Handbooks of the Mediæval and Italian Courts (by Messrs. M. D. Wyatt and J. B. Waring), where they are fully described.

The section of the Portrait Gallery, situated next to this Court, is devoted to the most celebrated characters of Italy, arranged in the order hitherto observed. The great nobility of expression seen in these heads will not fail to arrest the visitor, and to command his respect for the intellectual vigour which marks the creations of one of the most favoured spots—with respect to Art —on the earth's surface. We select from amongst them, Brunelleschi (131), Leonardo da Vinci (141), Michael Angelo (143),

Palladio (155), Canova (168), Paganini (170), Dante (173), Tasso (177), Alfieri (180), and Galileo (185 A).*

Bending our steps from this department to the junction of the nave and grand transept, we find the colossal statue of Rubens, by Geefs of Brussels, erected in the cathedral square at Antwerp, of which city Rubens was a native: the original is in bronze, and a fine example of the modern "Romantic" school of sculpture.   Advancing along this side of the transept, and continuing across the garden end, we observe several *chef-d'œuvres* of the late celebrated Italian sculptor, Canova: conspicuous amongst which are the well-known ".Graces" (125), the Dancing Girls (136, 137), Venus and Adonis (126), Mars and Venus (135), Venus emerging from the Bath (131), a group of Hebe and Paris, and a Magdalen (138).†

The finely designed equestrian statues of Castor and Pollux at this end of the transept, are cast from the originals in bronze, by San Giorgio, of Milan ; and form no unworthy pendants to the ancient Greek sculptures of the same subject, on the opposite side. The equestrian statue in the centre is the celebrated one of Colleone, modelled by Andrea Verocchio and cast by Leopardo. The original, in bronze, is erected at Venice, and has always been admired as one of those Renaissance monuments, in which energy and power are exhibited with unusual spirit and knowledge. Fringing the southern side of this transept are placed subjects from the extinct French school of sculpture, the earliest characteristic example of which may be seen in the Milo, by Puget (117).   Amongst the remaining statues we would notice the Bather, by Houdin (112), Julien's Amalthea (113), a Bacchante by Clodion (90), and Venus at the Bath (83), by Allegrini.†

At this angle of the nave and transept is placed

THE COLOSSAL FIGURE OF DUQUESNE.

The original of this fine bronze statue is erected at Dieppe in honour of the great French admiral, Duquesne. It was designed and executed by the sculptor Dantan, and is remarkable for the noble expression of the form and its spirited "Romantic" treatment at the hands of the artist.

From this statue, extending at the back of the extinct French school, will be found the fourth and last section of the Portrait

* Numbers of "Portrait Gallery."
† Numbers of "Handbook of Modern Sculpture."

Gallery, containing the illustrious men and women of France. Amongst them we remark Jean Goujon (196), Felibien (203), Rachel (216), Corneille (218), Lafontaine (220 A), Molière (221), Racine (225), Voltaire (233), Le Sage (230), Buffon (245), Massena (279), Ney (283), and the present Emperor Louis Napoleon (312).* In the centre of this compartment is another of Mr. Rimmel's fountains, executed from a design by Mr. John Thomas. The crystal basin, Parian marble figures, ebony pedestal, and natural flowers, harmonize excellently. At the back of this compartment, and corresponding to the German and English sculpture on the opposite side of the nave, is

THE COURT OF FRENCH AND ITALIAN SCULPTURE.

Amongst the very beautiful productions of the sculptor's art to be found in this Court, our space prevents more than a mere enumeration of some of the most remarkable, such as a colossal group of Cain (99), by Etex; "The Chase!" (No. 94), by Jean Debay, of Paris; Melpomene, by Rinaldi (154); Ishmael, by Strazza (160); Diana, by Benzoni (123); Esmeralda, by Rossetti (154); a child sewing, by Magni (148); and "the first cradle," by Auguste Debay (96), which deservedly occupies the place of honour in the centre, being one of the most charming works of modern sculpture; Venus disarming Cupid, by Pradier (116); Night, by Pollet (115); The Fates, by Jean Debay (93); Cupid in a Cradle (102), by Fraiken, a very prettily conceived and charming design in the style of the modern school; Venus with a Dove (103), by Fraiken; a Dancing Faun, by Luqueane (114), designed with much vigour; and, lastly, a Neapolitan "Dancer,"by Duret (98).*

At the back of this Court, on the garden side, are placed some remarkable historical statues of great interest: L'Hôpital (259) Chancellor of France under Henry II. (A.D. 1562), D'Aguesseau (269) Chancellor under Louis XIV.; Louis XIII. from the original in the Louvre, by Couston, a pupil of Coysevox. Louis XIV. (308 A), by Coysevox; † and the same monarch when a boy (308), from a bronze now preserved in the Museum of the Louvre. The remaining statue is that of Louis XV., by Couston (fils), an interesting work of the early part of the eighteenth century.

Quitting the Court, we continue our examination of the statues, which extend along this, the garden side of the nave, commencing

* Numbers of "Portrait Gallery."
† Numbers of "Handbook of Modern Sculpture."

next to Duquesne with Monti's admirable allegorical statue of Italy (159). The most notable of the succeeding subjects are the Prodigal Son (145), by San Giorgio ; David (147), by Magni, an artist whose studies of every-day life are remarkable for their truth to nature ; Cain (99), by Etex ; Geefs's Malibran (108) ; a colossal group of the Murder of the Innocents (142) ; a grand seated figure of Satan, by Lough (41) ; the Horse and Dead Knight (46), also by Lough ; a statue of Dargan, the munificent founder of the Irish Exhibition of 1853, by Jones (403*) ; an admirable statue, by Moore, of Sir Michael O'Loughlin, Master of the Rolls in Ireland, and the first Roman Catholic raised to the judicial dignity since the Revolution of 1688 (473).   Near to these is a characteristic and striking seated statue of Lord Brougham, by Papworth senior.

We now bend our steps to that junction of the Transept and Nave which is marked by a colossal statue of Huskisson, the first statesman to pioneer the way to Free-trade.   It is a noble work in the Classic style, by Gibson.

In this portion of the Transept are several works of the English School of Sculpture, amongst which may be particularly remarked a statue of Shakspeare (407B) by John Bell ; the Maid of Saragossa ; a very picturesque and vigorous ideal figure of a heroine, who has also inspired the pencil of Wilkie ; The Dorothea, so well known to the public by small copies in Parian marble ; a graceful statue of Andromeda, and Jane Shore.   All these specimens of Bell's power as a sculptor are on the north side of this part of the Transept.   Opposite to them will be found graceful statues of a Nymph (65) and Psyche (64), by Sir Richard Westmacott.   A Dancing Girl (50), by Calder Marshall, R.A.   The First Whisper of Love (49), Zephyr and Aurora (52), and an excellent portrait statue of Geoffrey Chaucer (53), the father of the school of English Poetry, also by Marshall.   Nearer the Nave is an ideal statue of Shakspeare by Roubilliac, cast from the original, still preserved in the vestibule of Drury-lane Theatre.   The colossal statue at the angle is that of the great German Philosopher, Poet, and Writer, Lessing, byRietschel of Berlin.   Along the centre of the Transept are placed the Eagle Slayer(6) by Bell, a work remarkable for its vigorous treatment ; the well-known and graceful composition, also by Bell, of Una and the Lion ; and the fine monument erected by the good citizens of Frankfort to the memory of the first printers, Gutenberg, Faust, and Schœffer.   The central statue represents Gutenberg,

* Numbers of "Handbook of Modern Sculpture."

who rests with an arm on the shoulder of each of his fellow-workmen. The original is by Baron Launitz of Frankfort, and is a creditable instance of the public spirit, which does not, after the lapse of centuries, forget the originators of The Press—that mighty power,—which performs at this day so grand a part in the governance, and for the benefit, of the civilized world. On our way towards the Queen's screen we pass several excellent works of statuary art, amongst which may be noticed, A Faun with Cymbals (66), by R. Westmacott, R.A., and a David (67*) by the same sculptor; and opposite to these Thorwaldsen's beautiful Venus with the Apple (218), and a fine statue of Erato (174), by Launitz.

LIST OF MODERN SCULPTURES.

No.
1. WILLIAM PITT, "THE GREAT LORD CHATHAM."
2. DR. JOHNSON.
2*. THE ELEMENTS.
3. A NYMPH PREPARING TO BATHE.
3 A. SLEEPING NYMPH.
3 B. THE GRACES.
3 C. APOLLO DISCHARGING HIS BOW.
4. THE TIRED HUNTER.
4 A. MATERNAL AFFECTION.
4 B. EVE.
4 C. EVE LISTENING.
5. UNA AND THE LION.
5 A. DOROTHEA.
6. THE EAGLE SLAYER.
6 A. JANE SHORE.
6 B. THE MAID OF SARAGOSSA.
7. ANDROMEDA.
8. THE INFANT HERCULES.
8 A. THE BROTHER AND SISTER.
9. SHAKSPEARE.
10. FLORA.
11. THE DANCERS.
12. SMALL MODEL.
12*. VENUS.
13. VENUS VINCITRICE.
14. FLORA.
15. CUPID DISGUISED AS A SHEPHERD-BOY.
16. A WOUNDED AMAZON.
17. NARCISSUS.
18. AURORA.
19. VENUS AND CUPID.
20. THE HUNTER.
21. PSYCHE BORNE BY THE ZEPHYRS.
22. HYLAS AND THE NYMPHS.
23. CUPID WITH A BUTTERFLY.
24. CUPID AND PSYCHE.
25. VENUS AND CUPID.
26. THE HOURS LEAD FORTH THE HORSES OF THE SUN.
27. PHAETON.
28. JOCASTA AND HER SONS.
29. WILLIAM HUSKISSON.
30. GRAZIA.

No.
31. BEATRICE.
32. CHRIST'S ENTRY INTO JERUSALEM.
33. THE PROCESSION TO CALVARY.
33*. CHILDREN WITH A PONY AND A HOUND.
34. THE EMIGRANT.
35. TWO BOYS WRESTLING.
36. A BATHING NYMPH.
37. SAMSON.
38. MUSIDORA.
39. MURDER OF THE INNOCENTS.
40. MILO.
41. SATAN.
42. ARIEL.
43. TITANIA.
44. PUCK.
44*. DAVID.
45. APOTHEOSIS OF SHAKSPEARE.
46. THE MOURNERS.
47. ANDROMEDA.
48. ULYSSES.
49. THE FIRST WHISPER OF LOVE.
50. A DANCING GIRL.
51. SABRINA.
52. ZEPHYR AND AURORA.
53. THE POET CHAUCER.
54. A NYMPH OF DIANA.
55. MERCURY.
56. SHAKESPEARE.
57. LAVINIA.
58. HIGHLAND MARY.
59. FLORA.
60. NARCISSUS.
61. PSYCHE.
62. HUMPHREY CHETHAM.
63. A BOY WITH A BUTTERFLY.
64. PSYCHE.
65. A YOUNG NYMPH.
66. A FAUN WITH CYMBALS.
67. AN ANGEL WATCHING.
67*. DAVID.
68. VENUS AND CUPID.
69. VENUS INSTRUCTING CUPID.
70. VENUS AND ASCANIUS.
71. "GO AND SIN NO MORE."

No.
72. PAOLO AND FRANCESCA.
73. INÒ AND BACCHUS.
74. CUPID AND THE NYMPH EUCHARIS.
75. A NYMPH.
76. A NYMPH ENTERING THE BATH.
77. A NYMPH ABOUT TO BATHE.
78. A HUNTRESS.
79. A NYMPH OF DIANA.
80. ZEPHYR WOOING FLORA.
81. A SHEPHERDESS WITH A KID.
82. PENELOPE.
83. VENUS AT THE BATH.
83 *. BACCHANTE.
84. THE NYMPH SALMACIS.
85. MODESTY.
86. CUPID.
87. CYPARISSUS.
88. A DOG.
89. CASIMIR PERRIER.
90. A BACCHANTE.
91. A NEAPOLITAN GIRL.
92. ADMIRAL DUQUESNE.
93. THE THREE FATES.
94. THE CHASE.
95. MODESTY AND LOVE.
96. THE FIRST CRADLE.
97. L'INGENUITÉ.
98. A NEAPOLITAN DANCER.
98 *. A NEAPOLITAN IMPROVISATORE.
99. CAIN.
100. A BATHER (LA BAIGNEUSE).
101. MILO OF CROTONA.
102. CUPID CRADLED IN A SHELL.
103. VENUS CARESSING HER DOVE.
104. CUPID CAPTIVE.
105. A WOMAN OF THE CAMPAGNA OF ROME.
106. A WOMAN OF THE RHINE.
107. PETER PAUL RUBENS.
108. MALIBRAN.
109. THE LIFE OF ST. HUBERT IN A SERIES OF EIGHT BAS-RELIEFS.
110. A DOG.
111. AN ITALIAN MOWER.
112. A BATHER.
113. AMALTHÆA.
114. A DANCING FAUN.
115. EURYDICE.
115.* CHARITY.
115 **. NIGHT.
116. VENUS DISARMING CUPID.
116*. A CHILD.
117. MILO OF CROTONA.
118. INNOCENCE.
119. VENUS.
120. A GIRL PRAYING.
121. CHARITY.
122. CUPID DISGUISED IN A LAMB'S SKIN.
123. DIANA.
124. PSYCHE.
125. THE THREE GRACES.
126. VENUS AND ADONIS.
127. ENDYMION.
128. NYMPH WITH CUPID.
129. PARIS.
130. TERPSICHORE.

No.
131. VENUS LEAVING THE BATH.
132. VENUS.
133. HEBE.
134. PSYCHE.
135. MARS AND VENUS.
136. DANCING GIRL.
137. DANCING GIRL.
138. THE MAGDALENE.
139. PERSEUS.
140. PERSEUS.
141. A FUNEREAL VASE.
141*. POPE CLEMENT XIII.
141†. A SLEEPING LION.
142. THE MURDER OF THE INNOCENTS.
143. THE DEAD BODY OF ABEL.
144. CASTOR AND POLLUX.
145. THE PRODIGAL SON.
146. DAVID.
147. A GIRL SEWING.
148. THE FIRST STEPS, OR THE ITALIAN MOTHER.
149. ITALY.
150. VERITAS.
150*. EVE.
152 MELANCHOLY.
153. EVE.
154. MELPOMENE.
155. HOPE.
156. ESMERALDA.
157. GREEK SLAVE.
158. THE MENDICANT.
159. AUDACITY.
160. ISHMAEL.
161. THE PERI.
162. MINERVA PROTECTING A WARRIOR.
163. A CHILD CHRIST.
164. THE CENTAUR CHIRON INSTRUCTING THE YOUNG ACHILLES.
165. PENELOPE.
166. HECTOR.
167. A NYMPH.
168. A GIRL BEARING FRUIT.
169. VASE.
170. POMONA.
171. MEDICINE.
172. A BACCHANAL.
173. FRANCONIA.
174. ERATO.
175. JOHAN GUTENBURG.
176. HOMER.
177. THUCYDIDES.
178. A GUARDIAN ANGEL.
179. MERCURY AND A LITTLE SATYR.
180. A CHILD PRAYING.
181. A BOY HOLDING A BOOK.
182. A BOY HOLDING A SHELL.
183. A DANAID.
184. A VICTORY.
185. A VICTORY.
186. A VICTORY.
187. A VICTORY.
188. A VICTORY.
189. A VICTORY.
189*. PUBLIC HAPPINESS.
190. THE MAIDEN ON THE STAG.
191. AN EAGLE.

No.
192. Four Long Bas-reliefs.
193. An Eagle.
193*. Two Stags.
193**. Two Youths, or Students.
194. Small Model of the Memorial
　　erected to Frederic the Great.
195. Equestrian Statue of Frederic
　　the Great, King of Prussia.
195*. The Cardinal Virtues.
195**. The History of Frederic the
　　Great.
196. A "Pietà."
197. Cupids riding on Panthers.
198. The Christ-Angel.
199. Morning, Noon, Night, Dawn.
200. Lessing.
201. A Madonna.
201*. A Violin Player.
202. A Nymph.
203. A Nymph.
204. Ceres and Proserpine.
205. Bavaria.
206. A Figure of Victory.
207. A Figure of Victory.
208. Four Angels.
212. A Knight.
213. Bellerophon with Pegasus and
　　Pallas.
214. Theseus and Hippolyta.
215. The Shield of Hercules.
216. Hope.
217. Venus.
218. Venus with the Apple.
219. Mercury.
220. Ganymede.
221. A Shepherd.
222. The Three Graces.
223. Love bending his Bow.
224. A Genius seated and playing
　　the Lyre.
225. A Vase.
226. The Triumph of Alexander.
227. Napoleon.
228. Lord Byron.

No.
229. Minerva adjudges the Armour of
　　Achilles to Ulysses.
230. Apollo playing to the Graces
　　and the Muses.
231. The Four Seasons.
232. The Genius of the New Year.
233. Cupid and Hymen.
234. Cupid and Ganymede.
235. Cupid and Psyche.
236. Cupid and Hymen.
237. Cupid bound by the Graces.
238. The Birth of Bacchus.
239. Love caressing a Dog.
240. Love making his Net.
241. Jupiter dictating Laws to Love.
242. The Four Elements.
243. Bacchus feeding Love.
244. Love awakening Psyche.
245. The Baptism of Christ.
246. A Guardian Angel.
247. Three Singing Angels.
248. Three Playing Angels.
249. Three Floating Infants.
250. Charity.
251. Christ Blessing Children.
252. The Virgin with the Infant
　　Christ and St. John.
253—260. Eight small Statues.
261. A Magdalen.
262. Hagar.
263. A Hunter.
264. A Hunter defending his Family.
265. The Shield of Hercules.
266. Telephus suckled by a Hind.
267. A Nereid.
268. A German Maiden with a Lamb.
269. Winter.
270. Diana.
271. A Flower Girl.
272. A Shepherd Boy.
　　The Zollverein.
　　Spain.
　　Paris.

Mixed with those exquisite productions of man that lie on either side of the visitor's path, Nature also bestows here some of her choicest treasures. We have still briefly to indicate the contents of

THE GARDEN OF THE NAVE.

The south end of the Palace and the south transept contain a selection of plants, consisting chiefly of Rhododendrons, Camellias, Azaleas, and other choice conservatory plants, most carefully selected ; in the south transept, especially, are arranged the finest specimens of these plants that can be seen. Opposite the Pompeian Court are placed two fine specimens of aloes, and, conspicuous opposite the Birmingham Industrial Court, are two Norfolk Island pines. Opposite the Stationery Court are two specimens of Morton Bay pine, as well as several specimens of *Telopea speciosissima* from Australia. Under the first transept may be noticed two remarkably fine Norfolk Island pines, presented by his Grace the Duke of Devonshire.

The garden facing the Egyptian Court is principally filled with palms ; and on either side of its entrance are two curious plants (resembling blocks of wood) called " Elephant's Foot ; " they are the largest specimens ever brought to Europe, and were imported from the Cape of Good Hope by the Crystal Palace Company. This plant is one of the longest lived of any vegetable product, the two specimens before the visitor being supposed to be three thousand years old. Before this Court will be noticed also two fine Indian-rubber plants—a plant that has latterly acquired considerable interest and value, on account of the variety and importance of the uses to which its sap is applied. Here will also be noticed an old conservatory favourite, though now not often met with, the *Sparmannia Africana*. Amongst the palms will be remarked many of very elegant and beautiful foliage, including the *Seaforthia elegans*, one of the most handsome plants of New Holland, and the *Chamœdorea elegans* of Mexico.. On the left of the entrance to the Egyptian Court will be seen perhaps the largest specimen in Europe of the *Rhipidodendron plicatile* from the Cape of Good Hope. Opposite the central entrance to the Greek Court, and in front of the beds, are two variegated American aloes. The beds are filled with a variety of conservatory plants, and have a border of olive plants. In front of the Roman Court will be observed, first, on either side of the second opening, two large Norfolk Island pines, presented by Her Most Gracious Majesty and His Royal Highness Prince Albert. The beds, like those before the Greek Court, are principally filled with Camellias, Rhododendrons, and Orange-trees, and are also bordered by several small specimens of the olive plant. Between the two foremost statues, at the angles of the pathway leading to the second opening, are placed two specimens of the very rare and small plant, which produces the Winter bark of commerce, and which is called *Drymus Winterii*. The garden in front of the Alhambra is devoted to fine specimens of the pomegranates. Having passed the Alhambra, we find the garden of the whole of this end of the building devoted to tropical plants, including a most magnificent collection of different varieties of palms.

Between the sphinxes are placed sixteen Egyptian date palms

(*Phœnix dactylifera*), recently imported from Egypt, and which owe their present unflourishing appearance to the delay that took place in their transmission, on account of the steamer in which they were conveyed having been engaged, on her homeward passage, for the transport of troops. Amongst the different varieties of palms, the following may be noted, either for their large growth or beautiful foliage : an immense specimen of the *Sabal palmetta* from Florida, and a fine *Sabal Blackburniana* ; also several fine specimens of the cocos, amongst which is the *Cocos plumosa*, reaching the height of thirty-five feet ; numerous specimens of the wax palm (*Ceroxylon andricola*), natives of Columbia, and the curious *Calamus maximus*, which, in the damp forests of Java, grows along the ground to an immense length, and forms with its sharp prickles an almost impenetrable underwood, are also here. The *Sagueras saccharifera* of India, noted for its saccharine properties, and the vegetable ivory palm (*Phytelephas macrocarpa*), deserve attention. The specimen of *Pandamus odoratissimus*, from Tahiti, is also remarkable, on account of its sweet smell.

Opposite the Byzantine Court, the garden is filled with different varieties of palms brought from South America, Australia, and the Isle of Bourbon. Before the Mediæval Court may be noticed two Norfolk Island pines, and close to the monuments at the entrance of the English Mediæval Court, are two funereal cypresses, brought from the Vale of Tombs, in North China. Close to the Norfolk Island pine, on the right, facing the Court, is a small specimen of the graceful and beautiful Moreton Bay pine. The garden in front of the Renaissance Court is filled with conservatory plants, consisting of camellias, azaleas, &c. On either side of the entrance to the Italian Court are two very fine American aloes, the beds here being filled with orange-trees, olives, and other greenhouse plants. In the garden, in front of the Foreign Industrial Court, will be noticed two fine Norfolk Island pines.

Having now explored the length and breadth of the ground floor of the Palace, we ascend the flight of stairs on the garden side (South), near the Great Transept, that leads to

THE MAIN AND UPPER GALLERIES.

The main galleries are devoted to the exhibition of articles of industry. It will be sufficient to give the visitor a general list of the objects exhibited, and to point out the situations in which the various articles of manufacture are placed. The gallery in which the visitor stands, together with its return sides, is devoted to the section of precious metals and the composed ornaments.

In the gallery beyond, towards the Sydenham or North end, are placed four hundred French and Italian photographs, illustrative of the architectural and sculptural arts of the periods represented by the several Fine Art Courts on this side of the nave ; the photographs being arranged in the order of the courts beneath, and as nearly as possible over the courts which they serve to illustrate. Here also will be found a fine collection of small works of art, consisting of statuettes, medals, and architectural ornaments, in like manner exemplifying the various styles from the Byzantine down to the Italian. In the north end, are works in porcelain and glass. In the north-western gallery (at the back of the Assyrian Court), space is appropriated to Oriental manufactures. Here also is arranged a collection of most interesting paintings, lent to the Crystal Palace by the Honourable East India Company. They are copies of some frescoes, found on the walls of a series of caverns at Adjunta in Western India, and were made at the instance of the Indian Government, by Captain Gill of the Madras army. The paintings represent scenes in the life of Buddha and of Bhuddhist saints, and various historical events connected with the rise and progress of the Buddhist religion in India. The date of their execution extends from about the Christian era to the 10th or 12th century ; and in style they closely resemble the contemporary works of painters in Europe, possessing nearly the same amount of artistic merit, and displaying the like absence of *chiar'-oscuro*, and the same attempt to copy, with literal exactness, the object represented. The collection is valuable, as affording the means of comparing the state of art in the East and in the West during the same period.

In the north-western Transept are specimens of photography. Nearer the Great Transept, in the same gallery, is arranged a valuable and interesting collection of photographs, illustrative of Oriental architecture, amongst which the Egyptian remains are particularly to be remarked ; whilst round the west end of the

Transept itself philosophical instruments, cutlery, and fire-arms will be exhibited. In the south-western portion of the gallery, leather and articles manufactured in India-rubber occupy the space to the centre of the south transept, from which point, to the end of the building, the gallery is devoted to perfumery and chemicals.

Along the south gallery, articles of clothing are displayed. Next to these are various miscellaneous articles, including work-boxes, fishing-tackle, and the thousand and one objects of general use. From this department, to the point in the gallery to which we first led the visitor, the space is appropriated to the department of substances used as food.

The visitor may now ascend the flight of spiral stairs in the central Transept, and step into the upper gallery, which is carried round the building, where a curious effect is produced by a series of circles extending along the building, and formed by the casting of each of the girders in four pieces. From this gallery a view is obtained of the whole length of the nave : and if we station ourselves at any angle of the north and south transepts, the nave will be seen to the greatest positive advantage. A still higher ascent up the winding staircase brings us to a gallery which extends round the centre transept itself ; and from this great height, nearly 108 feet above the level of the floor, a noble bird's eye view is gained, and the large Monte Cavallo groups below, as well as the modern Castor and Pollux, sink into comparative insignificance.

On the first small gallery, above the main gallery in the central transept towards the road, will be found an exceedingly interesting collection of drawings and models for the fountains in the Crystal Palace, which have been furnished by Mr. M. D. Wyatt, Mr. Owen Jones (the figures on whose designs were modelled by Signor Monti), Mr. John Thomas, Mr. John Bell, Baron Marochetti, Baron Launitz, and M. Hector Horreau. The models display much artistic treatment, and no small amount of inventive fancy.

Descending the staircase by which we reached the transept gallery, we regain the main floor of the palace, and proceed to the basement story, a portion of which, on the garden side, is appropriated to the exhibition of machinery in motion. This most important feature in the modern history of our country will receive, in the course of a few weeks, ample illustration. Passing on now, through the opening under the east end of the central transept, the visitor finds himself standing before—

View of Park and Gardens.

THE PARK AND GARDENS.*

Gardening, as an art, has flourished in all countries ; and has possessed in each such distinctive features as the climate, the nature of the soil, and its physical formation, as well as the character of the people, have created.   In the Gardens before us

* In the Park and Gardens, or in some part of the Palace, the band of the Crystal Palace, which is composed of sixty performers on wind instruments, and is the largest permanent band of the kind ever formed in England, will play every day ; in the summer, from three until six o'clock, and in the winter from one until four o'clock.   The members constituting the musical company, which has been collected from all parts of Europe, and includes Italians, Frenchmen, Hungarians, Germans, and Englishmen, have been selected from seven hundred candidates.   The most important instruments employed are the saxophones, the several kinds of which are capable of expressing the qualities and volume of sound produced by stringed instruments.   The musical director is Mr. Henry Schallehn.

two styles are seen, THE ITALIAN and THE ENGLISH LANDSCAPE.
A few words may be sufficient to describe the leading characteristics of both.

In Italy, during the middle ages, internal warfare confined men
to their fortresses, and no gardens existed save those "pleasaunces"
cultivated within the castle's quadrangle.   When times grew more
peaceful, men became more trustful, ventured forth, enjoyed the
pleasures of a country life, and gardening prospered.   In monas-
teries especially, the art received attention ; but it was not until
the beginning of the 16th century that a decided advance was
manifest, and then we have to note a return to the style of gardening that flourished in ancient Rome itself. Lorenzo de' Medici
possessed a garden laid out in the revived classical manner, and
this style, which is recognised as the Italian, has existed in Italy
with certain modifications ever since.   Its chief features are the
profuse use of architectural ornaments—the grounds being sub-
divided into terraces, and adorned with temples, statuary, urns,
and vases, beds cut with mathematical precision, formal alleys
of trees, straight walks, hedges cut into fantastic devices, jets
of water, elaborate rock-work, and fish-ponds dug into squares
or other geometrical forms.   Everything in these gardens
is artificial in the extreme, and in set opposition to the wild
luxuriance of nature ; and although the trees and shrubs are
planted with a great regard to precision, they are too frequently
devoid of all artistic effect.   During the last century, the Italian
style became blended with English landscape gardening, but without much success ; for the formality of the original style clings to
all Italian gardening at the present day.

English gardening does not seem to have been regularly cultivated until the reign of Henry VIII.; although, previously to his
time, parks and gardens had been laid out.   Bluff King Hal
formed the gardens of Nonsuch Palace in Surrey on a most magnificent scale, decking them out with many wonderful and curious
contrivances, including a pyramid of marble with concealed holes,
which spirted water upon all who came within reach,—a practical
joke which our forefathers seemed to have relished highly, for the
ingenious engine was imitated in other gardens after that period.
In this reign also were first laid out by Cardinal Wolsey the
Hampton Court Gardens, containing the labyrinth, at that period
an indispensable device of a large garden.   The artificial style in
James the First's time called forth the indignation of the great
Lord Bacon, who, although content to retain well-trimmed hedges

and trees, pleaded strongly in the interests of nature. . He insisted that beyond the highly-dressed and embellished parts of the garden should ever lie a portion sacred from the hand of man—a fragment of wild nature! He calls it "the heath, or desert." During Charles II.'s reign, landscape gardening received an impulse. It was in his time that Chatsworth was laid out, and that buildings were introduced into gardens. During his reign too lived Evelyn —a spirit devoted to the service of the rural genius. In his diary, Evelyn makes mention of several noblemen's and gentlemen's gardens which he visited, and some of which indeed he himself devised. His remarks convey an idea of the state of gardening during the reign of the merry monarch. "Hampton Park, Middlesex," he says, "was formerly a flat, naked piece of ground, now planted with sweet rows of lime trees, and the canal for water now near perfected; also the hare park. In the garden is a rich and noble fountain, with syrens, statues, &c., cast in copper by Fanelli, but no plenty of water. There is a parterre which they call Paradise, in which is a pretty banqueting-house set over a cave or cellar." It was under Charles too that St. James's Park was formed, a labour upon which the king employed Le Nôtre, the celebrated gardener of Versailles,—an artist of singular good taste, and with an admirable eye for the picturesque.

During the reign of William and Mary, Hampton Court was considerably improved. Some Dutch features were introduced into gardening, and vegetable sculpture, and parterres in lace, came into vogue.

To the Dutch must be conceded the earliest manifestation of a love for gardening, in Northern Europe—a feeling possessed by them even before the thirteenth century. The taste owed its origin, no doubt, partly to the general monotony of their country, partly to the wealth of their merchants, and partly to an extended commerce, which enabled the Dutch to import from the East those bulbous roots which have long been cultivated in Holland, and were once valued at fabulous prices. Dutch gardening soon acquired a peculiar character of its own. The gardens of Loo, laid out in the time of William III., were excellent examples of the symmetrical Dutch style; a canal divided the upper from the lower garden; the beds were cut in squares, and filled at various seasons of the year with tulips, hyacinths, poppies, sun-flowers, &c.; straight walks intersected the grounds, which were adorned with numerous statues, grotto-work, and fountains, some exceedingly whimsical and curious; the trees and shrubs were cut into devices, principally in pyramidical forms, whilst hedges separated the different parts of the garden, and were not allowed to grow above a certain height. Straight rows and double rows of trees constitute another characteristic of the Dutch style, and elaborate lace-like patterns for parterres were much in vogue during the latter part of the seventeenth century. The influence of this style upon English gardens may still be perceived in the clipped hedgerows and trees, green terraces, and now only prim, now magnificent avenues, so frequent in our country.

It would appear that from William down to George II., gardening in England suffered sad deterioration as an art. Formality prevailed to the most deadening and oppressive extent. The shapes of men and animals were cut in trees, and the land was threatened with a vast and hideous collection of verdant sculpture. Pope and Addison came to the rescue of nature, and ridiculed the monstrous fashion. Pope, in one of his papers in "The Guardian," details an imaginary set of plants for sale, including a "St. George, in box, his arm scarce long enough, but will be in condition to stick the dragon next April;" and a "quickset hog shot up into a porcupine by being forgot a week in rainy weather." Addison, in "The Spectator," says, "Our British gardeners, instead of humouring nature, love to deviate from it as much as possible. Our trees rise in cones, globes, and pyramids. We see the marks of the scissors upon every plant and bush." Pope himself laid out his grounds in his villa at Twickenham; and his gardens there, which still bear the impress of his taste, attest to his practical skill as a gardener.

The satire of these great writers contributed not a little to a revolution in English gardening. Bridgeman seems to have been the first to commence the wholesome work of destruction, and to introduce landscape gardening; and it is said that he was instigated to his labour by the very paper of Pope's in "The Guardian," to which we have alluded. But Kent, at a later period, banished the old grotesque and ridiculous style, and established the new picturesque treatment. He laid out Kensington Gardens, and probably Claremont. Wright and Brown were also early artists in the new style, and deserve honourable mention for their exertions in the right direction. The former displayed his skill at Fonthill Abbey, the seat of Mr. Beckford; Brown was consulted at Blenheim, where he constructed the earliest artificial lake in the kingdom —the work of a week. Nor must Shenstone, the poet, be forgotten. His attempt towards 1750, to establish the rights of nature in his own ornamental farm at the Leasowes places him fairly in the front rank of our rural reformers. Mathematical precision and the yoke of excessive art were thus cast off, the men and animals gradually removed themselves from the foliage, which was intended for birds and not for them, and nature was allowed a larger extent of liberty and life. She was no longer tasked to imitate forms that detracted from her own beauty without giving grace to the imitation ; but she was questioned as to the garb which it chiefly delighted her to wear, and answer being given, active steps were taken to comply with her will. Then came Knight and Price to carry out the goodly work of recovery and restoration. To them followed an early opponent but later convert, Repton, the gardener of Cobham Hall ; and as the result of the united labours of one and all, we have the irregularly-bounded pieces of water which delight the English eye, the shrubberies, the noble groups of trees, the winding walks, the gentle undulations, and pleasant slopes,— all which combined, give a peculiar charm to our island landscapes that is looked for in vain in fairer climates and on a more extended soil.

In the Crystal Palace Gardens, the Italian style has not been servilely copied, but rather adapted and appropriated. It has been taken, in fact, as the basis of a portion of our garden, and modified so as to suit English climate and English taste. Thus, we have the terraces and the architectural display, the long walks, the carefully cut beds, and the ornamental fountains : but the undulations of green-sward, that bespeak the English soil, give a character to the borrowed eilements which they do not find elsewhere. The violent juxtaposition of the two styles of gardening—the Italian, and the English— it may readily be conceived, would produce a harsh and disagreeable effect. To avoid the collision, Sir Joseph Paxton has introduced, in the immediate vicinity of the terraces and the broad central walk, a mixed, or transitional style, combining the formality of the one school with the freedom and natural grace of the other ; and the former character is gradually diminished until, at the north side of the ground, it entirely disappears, and English landscape gardening is looked upon in all its beauty.

The Crystal Palace and its grounds occupy two hundred acres, and it is of importance to note that, in the formation of the gardens, the same uniformity of parts is adhered to as in the building itself ; that is to say, the width of the walks, the width and length of the basins of the fountains, the length of the terraces, the breadth of the steps, are all multiples and sub-multiples of the

one primary number of eight.   By this symmetrical arrangement
perfect harmony prevails, unconsciously to the looker-on, in the
structure and in the grounds.   The length of the upper terrace is
1576 feet, and its width 48 feet ; the terrace wall is of Bath-stone.
The granite pedestals on each side of the steps, leading from the
great transept, are 16 feet by 24 feet.   The width of the central
flight of steps is 96 feet ; and this is also the width of the grand
central walk.   The lower terrace is 1656 feet long between the
wings of the building, or nearly one third of a mile, and 512 feet
wide, the basins for the fountains on this terrace being, as just
stated, all multiples of eight.   The total length of the *garden* front
of the wall of this terrace, which is formed into alcoves, is 1896
feet.   The large circular basin in the central walk is 196 feet in
diameter, and the cascades beyond are 450 feet long, the stone-
work that surrounds each cascade reaching to the extent of a mile.
The two largest basins for the fountains are 784 feet each in length,
having a diameter in the semicircular portion of 468 feet each.
Such are a few of the principal measurements connected with the
Palace Gardens, as these are seen on the surface.   But although
the work that is above ground may be recognised and calculated
with little trouble by the visitor, there is beneath the surface an
amount of labour and capital expended, of which he can with diffi-
culty form an accurate idea.   Drain-pipes spread under his feet
like a net-work, and amount in length to several miles ; he
treads on thousands of bundles of faggots which have formed his
path ; he walks over ten miles of iron piping which supply the
fountains for his amusement.

As the visitor quits the building, let him pause at the top of
the broad flight of steps leading to the first terrace, and notice the
prospect before him.   At his feet are the upper and lower terraces,
bordered by stone balustrades, the long lines of which are broken by
steps and projecting bastions.   Along these balustrades, at intervals,
the eye is attracted by the statues that surmount them.   Straight
before him runs the broad central walk, and, on either side of it,
on the second terrace, the ground is covered with green turf, now
relieved by beds filled with gay-coloured flowers, and hereafter to
be further heightened in effect by fountains throwing water high
up into the air.   As a side boundary to the foreground of this
picture, the wings of the building stretch out their blue colouring
and cheerful, light aspect, harmonizing with the rest of the scene.
Looking straight forward, below the level of the second terrace,
we see the site of the large circular fountain, surrounded by

architectural ornament, and white marble statues, which stand out
sharp and clear against the dark landscape beyond. On either side,
on a yet lower level, a glimpse will soon be caught of the glistening
waters in the two largest fountains, backed by embankments of turf;
and beyond these again, will be visible the waters of the large lake,
whose islands are peopled by monsters that inhabited the earth when
the world was young. To the right, and to the left, in the grounds, are
pleasant sloping lawns, dotted here and there with trees, and thickly

View from the Terrace.

planted shrubs; and then, beyond the Palace precincts, stretching
away into the far distance, is visible the great garden of nature
herself, a picture of rural loveliness, almost unmatched by any scene
so close as this to the great London city.   Undulating scenery
prevails : here it is rich with bright verdure, there dark with thick
wood : here, the grass field ; there, the grey soil, which, in the spring
time, is covered with the delicate green of young wheat ; and, in
the autumn, waves thick with golden corn.   Across the fields run
long lines of hedgerows, telling plainly of the country in which they
are found ; and in the very heart of all, the village church spire

shoots through the trees, surrounded by clusters of cottages, whose modest forms are almost hidden by the dark foliage in which they are nestled. The exquisite scene is completed by a long line of blue hills that ranges at the back of all.

Descending the steps we reach the first terrace, on the parapet of which are placed twenty-six allegorical statues of the most important commercial and manufacturing countries in the world, and of the chief industrial cities of England and France.

On each side of the great central staircase are statues representing Mulhausen, Glasgow, and Liverpool (to the right as we face the gardens), the two first by Calder Marshall, the third by Spence. On the left side are personifications of Paris, Lyons, and Marseilles, the first by Etex.

The next bastion, on the Sydenham side, is surmounted by statues of Spain and Italy, admirably executed by Monti ; the succeeding bastion forms a pedestal for the very characteristic figures of California and Australia by Bell. The staircase at this end of the terrace is ornamented at the first angle with representations of South America, by Monti, and of Turkey and Greece by Baron Marochetti ; the second group consisting of China, India, and Egypt, also by Marochetti.

The first bastion, on the Norwood side of the central staircase, supports allegorical statues of Manchester, by Theed, and Belfast, by Legrew. On the succeeding one are placed those of Sheffield and Birmingham, by Bell.

On each side of the staircase, at this point, are very excellent representations of the Zollverein and Holland, by Monti, and of Belgium, by Geefs.

The last group consists of a fine allegorical statue of the United States, by Powers, and of Canada and Russia, by Launitz.

All these figurative subjects are more or less composed in the style of the modern " Romantic " school of sculpture, and afford excellent illustrations of the character, nature, and chief occupations of the countries and cities they represent.

Proceeding in a northerly direction, we pass on until we reach a flight of steps, by which we gain the lower terrace, or Italian flower-garden. At the bottom of these steps are stone recesses, built under the terrace above, in which streams of water will fall from dolphins' mouths into bronze basins. Crossing the terrace by the path facing the steps, the visitor turns to the right, examining the flowers and the fountains, until he arrives at the central steps leading to the circular basin, from which point a most admirable view of the whole crystal structure is obtained. The deep recesses in the transepts, the open galleries, the circular roof to the nave, the height of the central transept, the great length of

South Transept, as seen from the Garden.

the building, and the general aërial appearance of the whole crystal fabric, produce an effect, which, for novelty, and lightness, surpasses every other architectural elevation in the world. Turning his back upon the building, the visitor beholds on either side of him green undulating lawns, beds planted with

The Arcade and Rosary.

rhododendrons and other flowers, and winding gravel walks. He now surveys the mixed garden, before mentioned, which extends

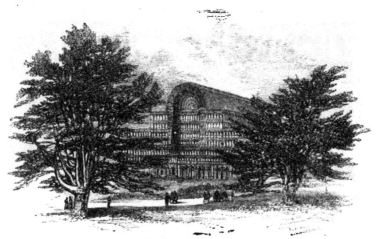

The Cedar Trees.

throughout the south side. To the right is a mound, surrounded by an arcade of arabesque iron work, around which innumerable roses are twined; and, to the left, two spreading cedar trees—of a kind familiar to this neighbourhood—attract attention by their thick, spreading, sombre foliage. Descending the steps, and walking round the broad gravel path, the visitor reaches the large circular fountain, which is destined to form one of the most brilliant water displays in the gardens, depending solely upon the water for its effect, and not at all upon architecture or sculpture; the water in this fountain will be made obedient to the hand of the artist, and shoot into the air, forming innumerable beautiful devices. Around the basin it will become a liquid hedge, whilst, in the centre and over the whole surface of the basin, it will be thrown up in sparkling showers, in all shapes, to all heights,— some breaking into misty spray at an elevation of seventy feet from the surface.

Round the basin of the fountain are white marble statues, copies from the antique, and of works by Thorwaldsen and Canova. Amongst them will be found the celebrated Farnese Hercules, the free and graceful Mercury by Thorwaldsen, and the Paris by Canova. Having made one half of the circle, the visitor, instead of proceeding down the central avenue, turns to the left, round the other side of the central fountain, and passing the first outlet finds his way through the second, and descends the steps into a walk which leads him to a smaller fountain.

Keeping to the left hand side, we make half the circle of this smaller fountain, and then enter upon a pleasant path, on the right side of which stands one of the noble cedar-trees before mentioned. We are now quitting the mixed Italian and English gardens for the pure English landscape. Trees wave their long branches over our heads, the paths wind, and art recedes before nature. Travelling for a short distance, we come to a junction of two roads. Selecting the left, we journey on through a path bordered on one side by trees, and on the other by a lawn, until we approach a valley at the bottom of which is a small piece of water, lying close to a thicket forming a pleasant summer shade. Leading out of this small piece of water is seen a large lake, which forms the second or intermediate reservoir for the supply of the fountains. Under the hand of Sir Joseph Paxton the lake is made to serve for ornament as well as use. Pursuing our way along the path chosen, and which is now open on both sides, we descend towards the east, and on either side of us are beds

THE STONE ARCADE.

filled with American rhododendrons. Our road takes us along the edge of the lake. Bearing to the right, we presently reach the junction of two paths. If the visitor turns to the left, he enters the Park which occupies this side of the ground, and forms not one of the least agreeable features of the place.

Quitting this Park, the visitor resumes his journey, continuing on the road which has brought him to the Park. He will shortly regain the Anglo-Italian gardens. Proceeding still to the left, he comes to a raised mound, or Rosary. Taking the right-hand path on the mound, we travel round it until we descend the path leading to the basin of one of the great fountains. Keeping to the right-hand side of the large basin, we proceed southwards along the gravel walk, at whose far end we find a stone arcade through which we pass, and over which, water rushing down from the temple, will, hereafter, form a sparkling veil as it falls into the basin. Having left the arcade, we turn to the right towards the building, and ascend the steps to the broad central gravel walk. We here behold the temples from which the water, of which we have just now spoken, is to flow. Now returning down the steps, we continue our road along the central walk, and skirt the margin of the right-hand basin, until we reach a flight of steps. These we ascend, and find ourselves upon an embankment called the Grand Plateau.

THE GEOLOGICAL ISLANDS AND THE EXTINCT ANIMALS.[*]

Taking our stand on the Grand Plateau, fifty feet in width, to which we have arrived, we obtain an extensive and general view of the geological illustrations, extending over twenty acres of ground. This ground is divided into two islands, representing successive strata of the earth, and by aid of the restorations of the once living animals that are placed upon them, presenting us, on the left, with the *tertiary*, and on the right, with the *secondary*, epochs of the ancient world.

Long ages ago, and probably before the birth of man, the earth was inhabited by living animals, differing in size and form from those now existing, yet having a resemblance in habit and structure, sufficiently close to enable us to institute a comparison that goes far to enlighten us upon the nature of these gigantic forms,

[*] The water for these islands will be supplied in the course of a few weeks.

whose bones, and sometimes even entire skeletons, are found buried in the earth, on the surface of which they once crawled; and it is from the study and comparison of these *fossil* remains that the vast bodies which the visitor sees before him have been constructed with a truthful certainty that admits of no dispute.

Quitting the plateau by an easy descent, we cross the bridge at the foot of it, and, on our right, divided by a watercourse, find a partial illustration of the Coal Formation. This has been admirably constructed by Mr. James Campbell, a practical engineer and mineralogist, and has been selected on account of the peculiar interest attaching to its strata of coal, iron, lead, and lime, all of which have helped so largely towards the prosperity of our commercial nation. The illustration commences at the lowest stratum with the old red sandstone, and ascends to the new red sandstone. The former is shown *cropping out* from under the mountain limestone and millstone grit above,—which in this case are thrown up, and display a great fault or break; whilst the displacement of the coal illustrates those faults, or troubles, as they are technically called, so often found in the working of that mineral, and which is caused by an upheaving convulsion of nature at some early geological period, as indicated by the stratum of new red sandstone above, which lies unconformably upon the dislocated masses below.

Proceeding still to the right, we come to a cleft in the limestone formation, in which will be found a reduced model of a lead mine, illustrating the characteristics of the lead mines near Matlock, in Derbyshire. The veins selected for illustration are called in mining phraseology the pipe veins and rake veins, the nature of the latter affording the opportunity of examining the interior, and walking through to the top of the limestone strata. Entering by the opening at which we have arrived, the visitor will at once have an opportunity of forming an idea of the general appearance and working of a lead mine, as a small shaft has been constructed, with a number of miners' implements exhibited, including, at the mouth of the shaft, a windlass, technically called a *stoce*. Having examined the interior, and proceeded through to the top of the limestone strata, we find ourselves again on the plateau, and by descending, regain the margin of the lake, where we face the *secondary* island.

The geological illustration immediately before us is the Wealden formation, so well known in Kent, Surrey, and Sussex, and formerly the great metropolis of the Dinosaurian orders, or the largest of gigantic lizards; these orders are here represented by the two *Iguanodons* (Iguano-toothed), and by the *Hylæosaurus* (the great Spiny Lizard of the Wealden), and the *Megalosaurus* (the Gigantic Lizard.)

Proceeding southwards, or to the right from the plateau, we come to the next stratum represented on the island. This is of the oolite period, so called from the egg-shaped particles of which the stony beds are composed, in which the bones of the great carnivorous lizard were discovered by Professor Buckland, called by him *Megalosaurus*, or Gigantic Lizard. Next in succession is the lias, formerly a species of bluish grey mud, but now

The Geological Island.

hard stone, containing an immense quantity of bones in the most perfect state of preservation, particularly those of the *Ichthyosaurus*, (Fish Lizard), and the *Plesiosaurus* (Serpent-like Lizard), with its long serpent-like neck, of which we see three specimens on the island. The two long-headed crocodiles, very like those of the Ganges, but double their size, together with the *Ichthyosauri* before mentioned, were the inhabitants of that part of England now known as Whitby, in Yorkshire, where the bones are found in perfect condition. The termination of this island represents the new red sandstone, remarkable for the numerous and varied footmarks found in it at different parts of our island, particularly at Liverpool, Chester, and in Warwickshire, where also have been found the bones and fragments of large frog-like animals, three of which are here built up by the creative mind and hands of Mr. Hawkins, under the guiding eye of Professor Owen. When the teeth of these animals were inspected by Professor Owen under a microscope, it was found that they had a singular labyrinth-like construction ; and the Professor accordingly gave to this particular inhabitant of the far-distant world the distinguishing name of *Labyrinthodon* (labyrinth tooth).

At this point the visitor will do well to retrace his steps, and to proceed again to the bridge, which will conduct him to the *third*, or *tertiary* island, where he will discover animals approaching more nearly in form and appearance the creatures of our own day. The most conspicuous is the Irish Elk with his magnificently branching

The Extinct Animals.

antlers. This restoration has been produced from an entire skeleton of the animal in the possession of the Company, and the horns are real, having been taken from the actual fossil. Another of the more recent wonders, meriting more than a passing glance, is the great wingless bird from New Zealand. The skeleton of this bird was theoretically constructed by Professor Owen from a small fragment of bone a few inches in length ; and when subsequently all the bones belonging to this bird arrived from New Zealand, proving its entire structure, the account they gave of themselves corresponded exactly with the account which the learned Professor, from deduction, had given of them in their absence.

Amongst the remaining monsters here represented may be noted the *Megatherium* (Great Beast), and the *Glyptodon* (Sculptured tooth Armadillo), from South America. The former is pourtrayed in his natural action of pulling down lofty trees for the purpose of more conveniently securing the foliage upon which he lived. The collection of extinct animals upon this island is as yet incomplete ; but at a future period the Indian series, and other large *Mammalia*, or suckling animals, including the *Mastodon* (the Breast-like tooth), the *Mammoth*, and the *Dinötherium* (Monstrous Beast), will be added to complete this instructive series.

The Cherry Tree.

Having surveyed these islands, the visitor returns to the Plateau.

Redescending from this point once more to the large fountain, he turns to the left, and proceeds round its margin until he arrives at the flight of steps on the opposite side. Ascending there, the path conducts him through a belt of young cedars which encircle the basins. A few steps further, and he arrives at the junction of two roads. Selecting that to the left, he will speedily gain the foot of the rosary, and the mound, at the top of which is

M

an ornamental arabesque arcade designed by Mr. Owen Jones.
He will here—as on the corresponding mound—find roses of every
variety, besides other plants which climb the sides and around the
roof of the arcade.   Looking from the opening in the arcade
towards the large circular fountain in the great central walk, he will
note, close to one of the projecting stone bastions, a fine cherry-
tree, which may be identified by the annexed engraving.   This
tree has an historical association in connexion with the Crystal
Palace; for it was beneath its shade that Sir Joseph Paxton
planned the magnificent gardens upon which we look.

View in Grounds.

Proceeding through the arcade to the right, we quit the mound
at the second outlet, and journey along a path, on either side of
which are flower-beds and groups of Rhododendrons and Azaleas.
Bearing to the right we reach the basin of a fountain.   Choosing
the left-hand side of this basin, we turn into the broad walk which
leads us by means of a flight of steps to the second terrace, making
our way to the south-end of which we shall reach an orangery in
the basement of the wing, where will be found a fine collection of
orange-trees—better known to Englishmen in general by their
delicious fruit than by acquaintance with themselves.   Leaving
the orangery for the terrace, we make our way by the steps to the
upper terrace.

At this point the visitor may either enter the southern wing of the building on his left, and proceed thence through the colonnade to the railway station, or advance by the right along the upper-terrace until he once more places foot in the building.

Having accompanied the visitor on his garden tour, we have now performed our office of cicerone through the Palace and grounds, and have brought before his notice the most beautiful and striking objects on his path. We have selected, both in the Palace and Park, a route which has enabled him to see the chief subjects of interest presented by our national Exhibition; but, as a reference to the plans will show, there are many other roads open, which may be explored in future visits; where our companion may wander as fancy guides him, within doors or without, through his eye feeding his spirit, whilst, as though in presence of the past and the distant, he looks on the imaged homes and works of the nations, or turns from the creations of human art and genius, to drink in delight, with wonder, from the strange or most familiar productions of bountiful, inexhaustible Nature. On every side, a soothing and ennobling contemplation, in which he may find rest from the fatigues, and strength for the renewed labours, of an active, a useful, and an enjoyed, if transitory, existence.

VIEW OF GREAT TRANSEPT.

LIST OF EXHIBITORS.

STATIONERY AND FANCY GOODS COURT.

Abbott, J. S., Specimens of Short-hand writing 9

Barritt and Co., Ecclesiastical Book-binding 22D

Baxter, G., Specimens of Oil Colour Picture Printing . . . 20

Boatwright, Brown, and Co., Specimens of Sealing Wax . . 9

Bohn, H. G., Printed Books . 15 and 16

Bradbury and Evans, Printed Books—Relief and Wave-line design engraved for Surface-printing—and the New Process of *Nature-printing* . . . . 6 and 29

Collins, H. G., Maps, Globes, &c., Lithographic Printing Press in action 25

Cook, T., Engraving . . .

Dolman, C., Printed Books . . 5A

Gilbert, G. M., Frames, Brackets, &c., Modelled in Leather .

Hyde and Co., Specimens of Sealing-wax and Stationery . 11

Haddon, Bros., and Co., Specimens of Type-Music; Stereotyping in various branches . . . 31A

Jarrett, G., Embossing, Copying, and Printing Presses . . 13A

Jones and Causton, Account Books, Stationery, and Printing . 22B

King, T. R., Paintings and Pencil Drawings 12

Knight and Foster, Mercantile Stationery 19A

Layton, C. and E., Specimens of Ornamental and Writing Engraving 13

Leighton, Bros., Chromatic Block Printing and Lithography . . 5

Letts, Son, and Steer, Articles of Stationery . . . 1 to 4

Marion and Co., A., Photographic Papers, Stamp-dampers; Sundry Fancy Articles . . . 24

Miland's Library, Plain and Ornamental Stationery . . 31B

Novello, J. A., Specimens of Musical Typography, Printing, and Illuminations . . . 22A

Pemberton, R., Books, Plans, &c. . 7

Pinches, F. R., Stamping Die Engraving &c., Crystal Palace Medal Press . . . 2A

Pope, H., Mercantile Stationery . 12A

Ralph, F. W., "Envelope Paper," Sermon Paper, and Business Envelopes 18

Roberson and Co., C., Artists' Colours and Apparatus . . 22C

Routledge and Co., G., Printed Publications 21

Saunders, T. H., Papers, hand and machine made, Bank note, Loan, Share, Cheque, and for Photographic purposes . . . 23

Shepherd, T. . . . .

Shield, Elizabeth, Portraits and Drawings in Pencil . . . 19

Smith, J., Stationery . . . 32A

Stanford, E., Maps, Books, and Stationery . . . .

Taylor and Francis, Ornamental Printing, Embossing, &c. . . 14

Tebbut, Rebecca, Desk, Stationery, &c. . . . . .

Williams and Co., J., Account Books of a Patent Construction . 8A

BIRMINGHAM COURT.

Allen, F., Articles of Gold and Silver Filagree Work, suitable for Presents and Testimonials .

Blews and Sons, W., Standard Weights and Measures, and Naval Brass-foundings .

Cope and Son, D., Electro, Nickel, and German Silver Spoons, &c. .

Greatrex and Son, C. .

Horsefall, J., Improved Music-wire, Covering-wire, Pins, &c.

Jennens, Bettridge and Co., Specimens of Papier Mâché manufacture .

Lingard, E. A., Coffin Furniture, Patent Cock, Seal Presses, Dies and Tools . . . .

Lloyd, W. B. . . . .

Parker, W., Jewellery, Gilt Toys, Masonic, and other Ornaments .

Peyton and Harlow, Patent Metallic Bedsteads . . . . -

Sutton and Ash, Specimens of Manufactured Iron . . .

Timmins and Sons, R. . . .

Warden and Co., J. . . .

SHEFFIELD COURT.

Addis, S. J., Carvers' and General Edge Tools . . . .

Butterly, Hobson, and Co., Scales, Scythes, &c. .

Cammell and Co., C., Springs, Steel, Files, &c. . . . .

Cocker, Bros., Sheffield Tools, and Mechanical manufactures. .

Fisher and Bramall, Specimens of Iron and Steel, Tools, &c.

Guest and Chrimes, Various Patent High Pressure and Fire-cocks, &c.

Jowett, T., Various kinds of Files,

and specimens of the manufacture of Steel .

Mappin and Bros., J., Cutlery; Silver and Electro-plated goods; Dressing-cases .

Nowill and Sons, J., Silver and Steel Cutlery .

Parker and Thompson, Assortment of Tools, &c. . . .

Smith, J. J. . . . .

Turton and Sons, T. . . .

Wilkinson and Son, T., Cutlery, Tailor's-shears, &c. . . .

MINERAL MANUFACTURES COURT.

Blanchard, Works of Art in Terra-Cotta . . . 3 and 5

Blashfield, J. M., Artistic Manufactures in Terra Cotta . 19 and 21

Browne, R., Various kinds of Tiles . . . 14 to 18

Bucknell, Jones, and Co. .

Burgon, J. T., Patterns of Gun-flints, German and Turkey Whetstones . . .

Doulton and Co., Stoneware Chemical Apparatus, Filters, Jars, Pipes, &c., Terra Cotta Vases . 10

Farnley Iron Co., Iron and Fire-clay Productions . . . 2

Finch, J., Patent Bricks, Tiles, and Bath-room Furniture . . 4

London and Penzance Serpentine Co., Obelisks, Monuments, Vases, Fountains, and various other Mineral Manufactures .

Minton, Hollins, and Co., Tiles, in Mosaic, Encaustic, Plain Venetian, Ornamented, Moorish, and other Styles .

Morgan and Rees, Implements, &c. used in the Manufacture of the Precious Metals .

Stevens, G. H., Glass and other Mosaic Work. . . . 20

Workman, J., Patent Brick and Cement. . . . .

HARDWARE COURT.

Adams and Sons, W. S., Victoria Regia Registered Baths, Furnishing Ironmongery .

Billinge, J. 25

Barlow, J., Household Utensils, &c. 22

Barringer and Co., D. C., Specimens of Moulding Sand, and Bronze Castings . . . 40A

Beverly and Son, J., Gas-Cooking-Stoves and Gas Meters. .

Benham and Sons, Ranges, Stoves, Fenders, Gas Cooking Apparatus, Tea Urns, Lamps . . . 41

Burney and Bellamy, Iron Tanks and Cistern . . . 40B

Chubb and Son, Patent Locks and Safes .

Clarke, S., Lamps, &c., of various kinds 16

Crook, E. and F., Improved Kitchen Range, Hot-plates, &c., Wrought Iron Lily .

Dufey and Sons, J., Patent Ranges, &c. 18

Hart and Sons, J., Patent Door Furniture, Ornamental Metal House-fittings . . . 32

Hill, J. V., Mechanical Tools . 12

Hulett and Co., D., Gas Apparatus 23

Huxham and Brown .

Jobson, R. . . . 1

Kent, G., Domestic Utensils . 14

Knight, T. and S. . 6A

Kuper and Co., Wire Ropes and Submarine Electric Telegraph Cables .

Lyon, A., Machine for Mincing, and for Manufacturing Sausages. 33

Masters, T., Various Patent Household Apparatus . . 4

Morewood and Rogers, Galvanized Tinned Iron, and Plumbic Zinc 29 & 31

Newall and Co., Patent Wire Rope and Cord . . . 2

Nye and Co., S., Patent Mincing Machine .

Parnell and Puckridge, Iron Safes, Locks, Doors, &c. . . . 5

Ralph and Co., C., Articles of Furnishing Ironmongery . . . 5A
Rickets, C., Gas Ranges, Stoves, &c. 5B
Robinson, Langton, and Co., Iron and Brass Ware, Tools, &c. . 12B
Russell and Co., J., Iron Tubing . 34
Russell and Sons, J., Gas and Locomotive Tubing, Patent Lap-welded Marine and Locomotive Tubing 42
Spiller, E., Bachelor's Tea Kettle . 6B
Stocker, Bros., Patent Beer Engines,

Lift-Pumps, Water Bottles, Pewter Goods, &c.
Thomas, R., Tools for various Trades 12A
Warner and Sons, J., Hydraulic Apparatus, Bells, Braziery Goods . . . . 15 to 19
Wenham Lake Ice Co., Refrigerators, &c. 21
Young, W., Spirit Lamps and Vessels, Gas Burners . . . 24
Zimmermann, E. G., Iron and Zinc Bronzes 5

FURNITURE COURT.

Alderman, J., Carriages and Furniture for Invalids . . .
Bateman, H., Specimens of Wood used in Pianoforte and Cabinet-work . . . . . 22 to 24
Bayly, J. D., Paper Hangings and Oil Paintings . . . 35 to 39
Betjemann, H. J., Patent Revolving, Rocking, Combination, and Reading Chairs . . 51
Betjemann, G. S., Patent Self-Fastening Centripetal Spring Bedstead; Indispensable Chair . 50
Blyth, Son and Cooper, Bedfeathers and Horsehair, Ottoman-Chair-Bedsteads 69
Baynes and Son, Specimens of dyed and cleaned Damask and Chintz furniture . . . 8
Box, J., Fancy Cabinet Furniture and manufactures . . 49A
Cooke, Hindley, and Law, Velvet-pile, Brussels, Kidderminster, and Berlin Carpets . . 8 and 9
Cox and Son, Ecclesiastical Furniture, Church Decorations, and Vestments . . 40 and 41
Crace, W., Chairs, &c., in carved Rosewood and Mahogany . 10 to 12
Day, H., Illuminated lettering of the 14th century . . . 44
Filmer, T. H., Cabinet Furniture, Easy-chairs, and Decorative Upholstery . . . 31A to 33A
Greenwood, J., Models of Glass Cases, fitted with India Rubber and Wooden Stops . . . 77

Harrison, R., Tapestry Work . 49
Horne, R., Pompeian and other Panelled Decorations . . . 29
Jackson and Graham
Loader, R., Household Furniture .
Lyle, J. G., Newly-invented Easy Chairs, Mattrass, &c. . . 74
Moore, J., Patent Moveable Glass Ventilator; Patent Respirator; and Specimens of a New System of Enamelling. . . . 42
Oliver and Sons, W., Specimens of Foreign Fancy Hardwoods . 17 and 18
Reed and Marsh, Library-table . 48
Rogers, W. G., Twenty Specimens of Carving in Wood . . 1
Smee and Sons, W., Cabinet Furniture . . . . 43A and 44A
Teale and Smith, Imitation Marquetry 46
Vokins, J. and W., Mechanical, Imitation Metal and other Frames 76
Wallis, J., Walnut Chess Table, ornamented with original paintings
Wallis, T. W., Specimens of Wood Carving 45
Wilkinson, Son and Co. . . 25 and 26
Winterbotham, A., Dacian Paper-hangings, Damasks, and Calicos. 4
Ward, J., Invalid Chairs for In-door and Out-door use . . . 49B
Webb, E., Coloured Damask, Damask Hair-Cloth, Hair Carpets, &c. 5
Yates and Nightingale, Painted and Embossed Table Covers, &c. .

MIXED FABRICS COURT.

Allan and Co., M. W., Silk Mercery and Drapery Shawls . . .
Bull and Wilson, Cloths, Fancy Silks, Cashmeres, &c. . . 12
Chironnet, V., Laces, Cleaned, &c. 43B
Dick and Son, J., Sewing Cotton on Reels 43A
Elliot, M. A., Irish Tabinet or Poplin
Farmer and Rogers, India, China, and Paisley Shawls . . 48
Faulding, Stratton, and Brough, Damask Table Linens . 39

Groucock, Copestake, and Moore, Lace and Muslin Manufactures . 42
Jay, W. C., Mourning Furnishing Goods 45
Leach, Broadbent, Leach and Co., Woollen Stuff and Fabrics . 22
Reid, J., Printed Muslins and Drapery
Simmons, W., Millinery, Fancy Bonnets, &c. . . . .
Swears and Wells, Articles of Hosiery 23

PRINTED FABRICS COURT.

Lewis and Allenby, Manufactured Silks, and Shawls . . . 7

Simpson, J. and J., Tapestry Damask for Curtains. . . . 18

MUSICAL INSTRUMENTS COURT.

Boosey and Sons, Various Wind Instruments, Patent Drum-stick, &c. 24

Brinsmead, H., Improved Pianoforte 42

Cooper and Son, J., Michrochordon Pianoforte 88

Challen and Son, Cottage Pianoforte 43

Distin, H., Various Wind Instruments, Patent Side Drum . 18

Greaves, E., Musical Tuning Implements 18

Hughes and Denham, Patent Grand Range Harmonichordon Pianoforte . . . . . .

Jones, J. C., Pianoforte . . 52

Köhler, J., Lever and other kinds of Brass Musical Instruments, of Patent Manufacture . . . 12

Levesque, Edmeades, and Co., Pianoforte 23

Marsh and Steedman, Cottage, and Michrochordon Pianoforte . 41 and 47

Moore, J. and H., a Cottage-Grand Pianoforte 35

Pain, W. G., Two Cottage Pianofortes . . . . 48 and 49

Peachey, G., Albert Piccolo Pianoforte 25

Sacred Harmonic Society, Model of Orchestra as arranged for the Oratorios of the Society . 65

Taylor, S. C., Two Concertinas .

Tolkien, H., Pianoforte . . 46

Ventura, A. B., Various Musical Instruments, Ancient and Modern . 4

SOUTH-EASTERN CORNER OF CENTRAL TRANSEPT.

Rimmell, E., Fountain of Sydenham Crystal Palace Bouquet.

NAVE.

Atkinson, J. and E., Perfumery, Soaps, and Toilet Furniture 9

Brown, S. R. and T., Specimens of Muslins and Laces, embroidered by Scotch and Irish Peasantry . 7

Forrest and Sons, J., Various kinds of Irish Lace and Embroidery . 12

Groux's Improved Soap Co., Household, Toilet, and Marine Soaps . 10

Hanhart, M. and N., Lithography and Chromolithography . . 3

Heath, J., Invalid Bath Chairs

Lancashire Sewing Machine Co., Sewing Machines . . . 5

Macdonald and Co., D. and J., Infants' Clothing . . . 4

Meyers, B., Walking Canes and Sticks. . . . .

Morgan, J., Wicks, &c., in Illustration of the manufacture of Candles. 8

Mechi, J. J., Dressing and Writing Cases, Cutlery, Pocket-books, &c. . . . . 2 and 17

Osler, F. and C., Crystal Glass Candelabra 6

Powell, J. H., Books and Maps, Hair Dye 16

Price's Patent Candle Co., Specimens of Candles, and of the Material manufactured; Extracts of Stearine and Oleine. . . 11

Rimmell, E., { Fountain of Eau de Cologne (S. E. End) Fountain of Toilet Vinegar (N. E. End) }

Robinson, H., Writing and Dressing Cases 15

Spiers and Son, Ornamented Works in Papier Mâché . 1

Thomas, W. F., Thomas' Patent London Sewing Machine . .

SOUTH WING.

IN OR NEAR THE REFRESHMENT DEPARTMENT.

Lipscombe and Co., Marble and Glass Fountains, &c. . . . . . .

NORTH WING.

DEPARTMENT FOR AGRICULTURAL IMPLEMENTS.

Barrett, Exall, and Andrews, Steam Engines, Agricultural Implements and Machinery

Barry, Bros., Specimens of Non-Poisonous Sheep-Dressing Composition. . . . .

Bigg, T., Dipping Apparatus for using Bigg's Patent Composition . . . . .
Boulnois and Son,
Buerell, C., Portable Steam Engine, Various Farming Machines .
Clayton, H., Various Patent Machines . . . . . .
Clayton, Shuttleworth, and Co., Steam Engine, Threshing Machine, Grinding-Mill . . .
Cogan and Co., ...
Cottam and Hallen, . . .
Croggon and Co., ...
Croskill and Son, W. . . .
Dray and Co., W. . . . .
Ferrabee, J. and H., Steam Engine, Grinding-mill, Mowing Machines, &c. . . . .
Garrett and Son, Models and drawings of Implements and Machines for Agricultural purposes . . . . . .
Haines, F., Shoes for Sheep, to cure Foot-rot, Foot-rot Powder .
Hart, C., Threshing Machines, with combined apparatus for Winnowing, &c. . . . . .
Hill and Smith,
Hornsby and Son, R., Portable

Steam Engine, Machines for Dressing and Drilling Corn
Howard, J. and F., Patent Ploughs, Harrows, Horse Hoes, &c.
Huxham and Brown, Three Millstones . . . . . .
Lyon, A., Machines for Cutting Vegetables . . . . .
M'Neill and Co.,
Nicholls and Co. Weighing and Chaff-cutting Machines, Scales, Weights and Measures, Corn Bruisers and Mills . . .
Pierce, W., , . . .
Ransomes and Sims, Agricultural Machinery, Steam Engines, &c.
Smith, S., ...
Smith and Ashby, Patent Haymaking, and Chaff-cutting Machines, Horse Rake, and Wheel Hand Rake, &c. . . . .
Smith, W., Improved Steerage, Horse-hoes, &c. . . . .
Stanley, W., ...
Tournay and Co., Wheels Manufactured by Machinery worked by Steam power . . . . .
Wilson, F. J., Patent Barrows .
Wilkinson, T., ...
Young and Co., C. D., . . .

EAST GALLERY, ADJACENT TO CENTRAL TRANSEPT.
DEPARTMENT FOR PRECIOUS METALS.

Acheson, W., Irish Jewellery and Ornaments, Antique and Modern 86
Benson, S. S. and J. W., Jewellery, Watches, and Plate . . 1 & 2
Biden, J. and F., Process of manufacture of Gold Chains, &c., Specimens of Seal Engraving, &c. 42
Chaffers, Jun., W., Coins, Medals, and Antiquities . . . 100
Connell, Mrs. M., Irish Bog Oak Ornaments 87A
Elkington, Mason, and Co. . 103 to 106
Forrer, A., Jewellery and Fancy Work in Hair . . . 87 & 88
Gorsuch, W. H., Precious and other Stones, with a Lapidary's Table, and Illustrations of the Process. 44
Goggen, J. 68
Hawkins, F.G.S., F.L.S., B. Waterhouse, Sketch Models of the Extinct Animals, &c. . . 42A
Holt, R. W., Work in Jet, Foreign Jewellery, &c. . . 131 & 132
Jackson, W. H. and S., Chronome-

ters and Watches, with Registered Improvements . . . 100A
Keith, J., Plate, &c., for Ecclesiastical Service . . . 44A
Mahood, S., Jewellery, Bog Oak Manufactures, &c. . . . 64A
Marriott, J. Glass Apiary, Humane Cottage Beehive, with Bees at Work . . . . . .
Marshall, E. S., Specimens of Goldbeating 62
Meyers, M., Jewellery, and Irish Bog Oak Ornament . . . 88A
Restell, R., Clocks, Watches, Plate, Jewellery, &c. . . . . .
Staight, T., Manufactures in Ivory, Pearl, Tortoiseshell, &c. . . 46
Steinitz, Bros., Parquetose Flooring, Ivory Carved, Wood Mosaic.
Vieyres and Repingon, An Astronomical Clock . . . 100B
Watherston and Brogden, Gold Chains and Miscellaneous Jewellery . . . . 101 & 102
Waterhouse and Co., Ancient and Modern Irish Jewellery . 65 & 66

SOUTH-EASTERN GALLERY.
DEPARTMENT FOR SUBSTANCES USED AS FOOD.

Batty and Co., Pickles, Preserves, Sauces, and Oilmen's Stores . 15 & 16

Dunn and Hewett, Cocoa, Coffee, Extracts and Spices . . . 5

Edwards, Bros, Preparations of Farinaceous and other Food . . 12

Fry and Sons, Cocoa, its Varieties of Growth and Manufacture . 17

Glass, G. M., Isinglass, Gelatine Lozenges, and Jujubes . . 12B

Gunter, R., Bride Cakes and Confectionery 20

Horniman and Co., Tea as Imported free from Artificial Colouring . 10

Kent and Sons, Bordeaux Wine Vinegar 12A

Lea and Perrins, Sauces, Chemical Drinks, &c. 18

Paris Chocolate Co., Cocoa and its various manufactures . . .

Phillips and Co. Tea and Coffee in all their various kinds . . . 11

Slee, T. P. and C. B., Mustard in the Seed and Manufactured. Blue for Laundry purposes . . . 6A

Turner, G., Wedding and other Cakes 9

Vickers, J., Russian Isinglass in Shapes 18A

White, G. B., Cocoa, and Chocolate in their various stages of preparation . . . . .

DEPARTMENT FOR MISCELLANEOUS ARTICLES.

Austin, J., Patent Line . .

Cave, A., Fancy Articles, Workboxes, &c. 14

Davis, Mrs. Cigars and Tobacconists' Goods in General . . 12A

Davis, J. J., Seal Engraving, Copying and Embossing Presses . 16

Farlow, C., Fishing Tackle . 12

Inderwick, J., Fancy Goods, more particularly in connection with Smoking, Tobaccos, &c. . . 21 & 22

Jones, B. C., Cigars of every description . . . . . 1 & 2

Kite, J., Patent Ventilating and Smoke Curing Apparatus, illustrated by experiment . . 3A

Latour, Rateau and Co., Dyed and Cleaned Goods . . . '

Lillywhite, Bros., Articles connected with the Game of Cricket 9

Marsland, Sons, and Co., Fancy Work and Cotton. . . . 5 & 6

Muggleton, W. H., Linen Stamps, Marking Ink, &c. . . 4

Nixey, W. G. Patent Revolving Till, Blacklead, &c., Dyes, Varnishes, &c. 10

Phillips and Co., Pipes, Stems, and Cigar Tubes 17

Rymer, S. L. 4A

DEPARTMENT FOR FINE LINENS AND DAMASKS.

Hollins, E., Patent Shirting . .

Russell, H. and G., Specimens of

Sail Cloth of English and American manufacture . . .

SOUTH GALLERY.

DEPARTMENT FOR CLOTHING.

Berni and Meillard, Velvet and Beaver Hats of all descriptions . 4

Brook, Bros., J. . . . . 39 & 40

Caplin, Mme. R. A., Medical Corsets, Belts, Supports for Invalids, &c. 8

Capper and Waters, Shirts of various fashions . . . 12 & 14

Carrol, Bridget, Various Articles of Dress in Lace . . .

Carter and Houston, various Kinds of Improved Corsets . . 33

Coles, W. F. Newly Invented Socks, of various kinds . . 16A

Cooper and Fryer, the Gorget Patent Shirt, Elliptic Collars, &c. .

Daily and Co., Specimens of Dyeing and Cleaning Silks, &c. . 5

Dando, Sons, and Co., Hats and Caps Manufactured for lightness 16

Davies, J., Fashionable Riding Habit 36A

Eason, J., Ready-made Linen, French flowers, &c. . . 24 to 26

Ellwood and Sons, J., Air-

Chamber Hats, &c., for Warm Climates 34

Gaimes, Sanders, and Nicol, Pliant Ventilating Hats . 19 & 20

Glenny, C., Balbriggan Cotton Hosiery 10A

Grundy, T., Easy Boots of a New and Improved Manufacture . 32

Hawkins, Mrs., Corsets and Belts . 32A

Hayward and Co., Embroidered Cloth, Silk, Berlin Cloth, &c. . 32B

King and Co., W., Silks, Satins, Velvets, Woollen Manufactures, Cambrics, Linen, Haberdashery, &c. 2

Marion and Maitland, Corsets, Medical Supports, &c. . . 36

Nicoll, B., Specimen Shirts . 18A

Nicoll, H. J. and D., Specimens of the Fashion, Patented and Registered Articles of Dress and Personal use . . . 17 & 18

Paine, H. and Co., Trousers . .

Philps and Son, Ladies and Children's Clothing and Hosiery 25A & 26A

Price and Co., Waterproof and Air-proof Goods . . . .

Rumble, Mrs., Surgical Bandages, Supports, &c. . . . .

Smith, Mrs. J., Corsets and Socco-pedes, Elastic or Silk Boots .

Smith, Julia, Corsets . . . 35A

Stray, F., and Co., Specimens of Embroidery and Articles of Fash-ionable Dress for Gentlemen . 28

Stroud, M. and D., Articles of Ho-siery, &c. 6

Stuart, J. K., Patent Ventilating Hats 35B

Thompson, Miss S. C., Widows' Caps 8A

Thresher and Glenny, Under-cloth-ing for Warm Climates, Notting-ham Hosiery 10

Upton and Co., W., Specimens of English and Foreign Leathers, and Leather Mercery . . . 30

Watkins, W., Military and other Clothing 1

Whitelock and Son, Articles of Hosiery 41

Williams and Son, R., Umbrellas, Parasols, Whips, Canes, &c. 21 & 22

Wright, E. J., Corsets, &c. . . 85

SOUTH END OF BUILDING.

DEPARTMENT FOR STAINED GLASS, &c.

Nosotti, C., Large Looking Glass in Solid Carved Florentine Style of Frame . . . . .

Waites, W., Three Stained Glass Windows . . . . .

SOUTH-WESTERN GALLERY.

DEPARTMENT FOR MISCELLANEOUS ARTICLES.

Allaire, Réné, Specimens of Dyeing and Cleaning. . . . 34A

Barnett, B., Specimen of Old Paint-ing Restored . . . .

Bartlett, J., Patent Compressed Cricket Bats. 36A

Burningham, C., Assortment of Goods in Papier Mâché . . 47

Carles, H. R., Gentlemen's Head-dresses and Perukes . . 32

Child, W. H., Specimens Brushes manufactured in Ivory, Bone, Tortoiseshell, and Wood . .

Collings, J., Tailor's Registered Arm-pad 39

Cowvan, B. and S., The Canton, or Quadrilateral Strop . . . 38

Cullingford, W., Various kinds of Netting 53A

Curtis and Son, M. I., Pianoforte-strings, Wire-screws and Pins .

Dillon, A., Specimens of Orna-mental Writing . . . .

Farley, H., Models of Naval Archi-tecture and Implements . .

Foot, Mary, Artificial Flowers, Head-dresses, &c. . . . 49

Freckingham, Mrs. E. Specimens of Fancy Work . . . 87

Giles, J. A., Specimens of Portrait Painting 56

Gittens and Allkins, Patent De-tector Tills and Base Coin Detectors 27A

Grujeon, A., Cases of Plants, ar-ranged in Botanical Order . . 89A

Hack, R., Harmonicon and Flute Flageolet 30

Helfrick, F., An Invention to Navi-gate the Air, invented by W. Bland, Esq., N. S. W. . . . 29A

Hodges and Turner, Various kinds of Elastic Fabrics. . . . 81A

Holliday, R., Self-generating Gas Lamps, Chemicals, &c. . . 81

Hyams, M., Cigars, Tobacco, and Illustrations of their Manufac-ture 29

Jackson, W., Wirework Mountings for Whips, &c. . . . 72

Joyce, F., Percussion Gun-caps, Primers, Waddings, &c. . . 27B

Judson and Son, D. Dyewoods and General Drysalteries . .

Lee, Thomas, Waterproof and Air-proof Goods 28A

Levin, L., Glass Beads, Real and Artificial Coral, &c. . . 82A

Loysel, M., Newly-invented Ma-chines for Making Coffee . 41 & 42

Maynard, J., Wire, &c., used in the Manufacture of Pianofortes . 36

Mead and Powell, Toys, &c., Fancy Cabinet Work . . 43 & 44

Noden, J., Hair-Dye, with Speci-mens of its Application . . 49B

Olin, L., Purses made by Machi-nery . . . . .

Parker, J., Stag's-horn Umbrella Stand 47A

Pierotti, H., Wax Dolls and Figures for Hairdressers . . . 40A

Ralph and Son, Articles of Gentle-men's Fashionable Dress .

Ramage, R., Fair's Patent Venti-lators 89B

Read, T., Specimens of Ornamental Writings, Embossing, Household Decoration, and Lithography . 27A

Revell, J., Ornamental Leather-work, and Implements, and Materials used 88A

Riddell and Co., W., (Anglo-Continental Co.) . . . .
Roe, F., Models of Fountains, Jets d'Eau, Valves, &c.
Salmon, L 35A
Samuel, M., Foreign Shells, Corals, and China 58
Sanders, W., Modelling in Leather 82B

Sangster, W. J., Parasols, Umbrellas, &c., of various kinds . 84
Saunders, J., Specimens of Teas and Coffees . . . 40
Saunders, R. Fast-dyed Woollen Goods and Dye Detector . .
Walden, H., Variegated Linen-Baskets 55

DEPARTMENT FOR PERFUMERY.

Eason, R., Hair Perfumery, Combs and Brushes . . . .
Higgins, J., Distilled Essences for Perfumes 6
Lewis, J., Perfumes, Soaps, and Toilet Furniture . . .

Saulson, M., Soaps, Essences, Pomatums, &c. 5
Sturrock and Sons, Perfumery, and Toilet Furniture . . . 3 & 4

DEPARTMENT FOR CHEMICALS.

Allshorn, F., Homœopathic Medicine Chest, Medicines, Works, &c. 4A
Andrew, F. W., Cemented China and Glass, Articles of Toilet Furniture 6
Blundell, Spence, and Co., Assortment of Painter's Colours . 5A
Burton and Garraway, Cudbear, Orchil, and Indigo Dyes . 4
Electric Power Light and Colour Co., Electric Colours . . 2A
Field, J. C. Specimens of Wax, Candles, Sealing Wax, &c. . 7
Gibbs, D. and W., Fancy and other Soaps 1A
Jones and Co., Orlando, Specimens of Starch from Rice . . 3

King, W. W., Effervescent Citrate of Magnesia 4B
Prockter, Bevington, and Prockter, Inodorous Glue . . . 6A
Rottmann and Co., G., Sodawater Machines and Filters . .
Reeves and Sons, Artists' Water Colours and Implements . . 0
Rose, W. A., Oil and Grease, for Burning and Machinery, Varnishes, Paints, &c. . . 8
Walker and Stembridge, Gums, Glues, Dyes, and Chemicals .
Williams and Fletcher, Colours and Chemicals . . . .

DEPARTMENT FOR LEATHER.

Blackwell, S., Assortment of Saddlery and Harness, patent and otherwise 40
Brown, J., India Rubber Beds, Sofas, Chairs, and Marine Spring Bed . . . . .
Cant and Sons, G. W., Ladies and Gentlemen's Boots and Shoes of all kinds 14
Clarke, C. and J., Manufactures from the Angora and Sheep Skin, Boots, Shoes, and Slippers 21 and 22
Davis, Mrs. A., Saddlery, Harness, and Horse Clothing . . 12
Deed, J. S., Morocco Leathers of Various Kinds, Dyed Sheep and Lamb's-wool Rugs . . 24
East and Son, T., Specimens of Leather and Manufactures from the Skin of the Sheep . . 4
Ford, A. F., Boots and Shoes . 28
Gutta Percha Co., the West Ham, Articles manufactured in Gutta Percha, under Letters Patent .
Gottung, J. B., Two sets of Harness, worked with Peacock-quills; Covers and Mats of Peacock-work 19

Hall, J. S., Models of Boots manufactured for the Royal Family and Nobility . . . 10
Haines and Nobes, Mill-bands and other Articles of Leather Manufacture 26
Hall and Co., Leather-Cloth Boots and Shoes, Goloshes, &c. . 20
Jeffs, R., Furs of the Arctic and Cold climates . . . 6
Jones and Waters, Fancy Leathers used in the Manufacture of Hats, Caps, &c. 28
Marsden, C., Ventilating Boots, Shoes, Goloshes, &c. . 37 & 38
Maxwell and Co., H., Spurs and Sockets 10A
Newton, T., Harness and Horse appointments generally .
Norman, J. W., Boots and Shoes, &c. 28A
Oastler and Palmer, Specimens of Tanned Skins . . . 34 & 36
Preller, C. A., Patent Leather Machine Bands, &c. . . 18
Roberts, E. B., Manufactures from the Beaver, and various other Skins 0

Swaine and Adeney, Whips and Riding Canes of all kinds . . 32
Southgate, G., Solid Leather Portmanteaus 16A
Urch, H., Saddlery 6A
Wansbrough, J., Garments Manufactured from the Patent Para-India Rubber Cloth . . . 39

Watson, C. J., Utilis Portmanteau 30A
White, J. C., Harness, with White Patent Tugs 16
Wilson, Walkden, and Co., Prepared Sheep Leather . . . 35A
Wright, R., Patent Boots and Shoes . . . . . .

DEPARTMENT FOR INDIA-RUBBER.

Edmiston and Son, India Rubber Clothing, Ornamental Objects, in Gutta Percha and India Rubber . . . . . 19 & 20
Goodyear, C., Articles Manufactured from India-Rubber . . 1 to 12

Grueber and Co., Patent Asphalte Sheathing and Dry Hair Felt .
Mackintosh and Co., India-Rubber, native, and manufactured, with illustrations of the process . . . . . . 13 to 18

WEST GALLERY, ADJACENT TO CENTRAL TRANSEPT.

DEPARTMENT FOR PHILOSOPHICAL INSTRUMENTS.

Bailey, W. H., Medical Instruments, Invalid Supports, &c. . 87
Beard, Jun., R., Daguerreotype and Photographic Pictures. Stereoscopes, &c. . . . 33 & 34
Bermingham, Esq., T., Maps, Plans, &c. 48A
Caplin, M.D., J., Medical Gymnasia, Instruments, and Furniture for the Cure of Deformities . . 47A
Claudet, A., Daguerreotype and Stereoscopic Portraits
Coles, W., Patent Trusses
Colt, Colonel S., Patent Repeating Firearms . . . 91 & 92
Cronmire, J., M. and H., Mathematical and Nautical Instruments 60
Deane, Adams and Deane, Fire Arms
Elliott, Bros., Optical, Mathematical, and Philosophical Instruments 29
Elliot, J., Daguerreotype and Stereoscopic Portraits . . 40
Grossmith, W. R., Artificial Eyes, Limbs, and other Productions of Surgical Mechanism . . . 27
Harnett, W., Dentistry and Articles used in Dental Surgery
Hennah and Kent, Photographs . 49
Hobson, T. 88A
Hogg, R., Photographic Portraits, Landscapes, &c. . . . 40A
Horne, Thornthwaite, and Wood,

Photographic Cameras, &c., Pictures, Medical Electro-Galvanic Machine 48
Laroche, M., Photographic Pictures.
Mayall, J. E., Photographic Pictures 31
Miles, E., Artificial and Mineral Teeth, Gums, and Palates . . 37
Newson, H., Patent Wire Trusses 49A
Novra, G., Cutlery, Articles in Electrotype 11
Pottinger, C. R., Photographic Apparatus, Stereoscopes, &c. 1 & 2
Potter, J. D., Scientific and Philosophical Instruments . . 58A
Prince and Co., Models of Inventions
Read, R., Agricultural and Horticultural Machines, Surgical Instruments, &c. 41
Reid, W., Instruments and manufactures in connection with the Electric Telegraph . . . 47
Smith S., Trusses, Medical Supports, &c.
Statham, W. E., Philosophical Instruments in connection with Chemistry 58
Stidolph, W., Educational Instruments for the Blind . . . 38
Sharpe, T., Photographic Portraits 50
White, J., Patent Trusses, Belts, Surgical Supports, &c. . . 30

DEPARTMENT FOR PRINTED BOOKS, ETC.

Kent, W., Printed Books .

Tweedie, W., Temperance Books and Publications . . . .

NORTH-EASTERN GALLERY.

DEPARTMENT FOR CHINA AND GLASS.

Aire and Calder Bottle Co., Specimens of Glass Bottle Manufacture . . . . . 33 & 34

Bourne and Son, Patent Stone-Ware Bottles, Jars, Vases, &c. . 15

Brace and Colt, Manufactures of the "Serpentine" stone . .

Clarke, Miss C., Antique China, Point Lace, &c. . . . 65 & 66

Claudet and Houghton, Glass Shades and Photographic Glasses

Copeland and Son . . . .

Goode and Co., T., China, Glass, China Lace Figures, imitation Majolica Ware . . . 6

Green, J., Useful and Ornamental China, Glass, and Earthenware. . . . . 37 to 40

Hetley, H., Glass Shades and Cases 28

Hetley and Co., J., Glass-shades Window and Horticultural Glass 36

Kerr, Binns, and Co. . . . 41

Litchfield, S., Ancient Furniture, China, Clocks, Candelabra, Bronzes, &c.

Lockhead and Co., J., Patent Perforated Glass, Specimens of Glass, and Glass Manufactures . 13

Roberts, J., Patent Invention for Cooling Drinks and Edible Matters; Specimens of Terra Ferrum 10

Sinclair, C., Glass and China . 11A & 12A

BASEMENT.

DEPARTMENT FOR MACHINERY.

Beecroft Butler and Co. . .

Bellhouse and Co., E. T. . .

Bernard, J. .

Birmingham Patent Iron and Brass Tube Company . .

Bradbury and Evans . .

Burch, E. J. .

Calvert, F. C. .

Collins, H. H. .

Coltman, W. .

Condie, J. .

Dalgetty, Ledger, and Co. .

Dering, G. E. .

Dunn, Hattersly and Co. .

Galloway, W. and J. .

Gent and Co., G. .

Goodall, H. .

Goodfellow, B. .

Grout, J. .

Hanson and Chadwick .

Harrison and Sons, J. .

Hill, W. .

Hughes and Denham .

Hughes, R. and T. .

Lister and Co. A. .

Lloyd, Jun., G. B. .

Lloyd, G. .

Lomas, Fromings, and Sykes . .

Muir, G. W. .

Mansell, T. .

Mason, J. .

Manlove and Alliott .

Moseley and Co., J. .

Onions, J. C. .

Percy, W. C. S. .

Piper and Co. .

Preston, F. .

Quick, J. V. .

Ramsbotham, J. .

Reade, Spencer, and Co. .

Renshaw, G. P. .

Robinson and Co., H. O. .

Richmond, S. .

Samuelson and Co. M. .

Shand and Mason .

Smith, B. and J. .

Snowden, F. W. .

Taylor, T. .

Walker and Hacking .

Walsh and Co., A. J. .

Warner and Sons .

Whitworth and Co. .

Wright and Co. .

Williams, W. .

DEPARTMENT FOR CARRIAGES.

Corben and Sons, Carriage upon improved principles . .

Hedges, W., Patent Curriculum .

Hoadley, A. and S., A Carriage of First-class Manufacture . .

Holmes, H. and A., Two Improved Four-wheeled Carriages .

Kinder and Co., Light Dog-Cart Phaeton .

Kesterton, E., A Dog-Cart of Improved Construction, with Patent Shaft, &c. . . . .

Lenny, C., Carriage of the latest Plan . .

Mason, W. H. .

Meaden, M., Four-wheeled Carriage .

Offord and Co., R., A Carriage .

Starey, T. R., Cottage Dog-Cart .

Thrupp and Co., C. J., A Four-Wheeled Carriage .

Tudor, W. H., Barouche, Park Phaeton.

EXHIBITORS NOT CLASSED.

Boorer, R., Slate Tables in imitation of various Marbles . . .

Cross and Co., J. W., Pails and Patent Fire Engines . . .

Camolera, M. de, Specimens of Flower Painting on Porcelain .

Kennard and Co., R. W., Cast Iron Gates and Railing made for the Peruvian Government. Vases and Ornamental Castings. The Cast Iron Garden Chairs in the Grounds . . . . .

McCrea, H. . . . . .

Merryweather, M., Fire Escapes, Fire Engines, and Implements .

Stewards and Co., Statue in Portland Stone . . . . .

Taylor, Mrs. A. M. N., Various Specimens of Sea Weed . .

Wood and Jerry, Carved and Engraved Shells . . . .

Wilson, J., Statuette in Parian Marble . . . . .

Wilkinson, Letitia, a Churn on Stand . . . . .

BRADBURY AND EVANS, PRINTERS, WHITEFRIARS.

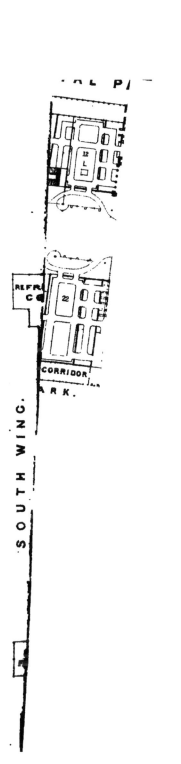

SINCE this Handbook was sent to press some of the objects mentioned have received a new position; but the

in the book.

June 2nd, 1854.

LARDNER'S MUSEUM OF SCIENCE & ART.

Weekly Numbers at 1d., Monthly Parts at 5d., Quarterly Volumes at 1s. 6d.

EDITED BY DR. LARDNER.

ILLUSTRATED BY NUMEROUS ENGRAVINGS ON WOOD.

CONTENTS OF

VOLUME I., *price 1s. 6d., in handsome boards.*

Part I., price 5d.
1. The Planets; Are they Inhabited Globes?
2. Weather Prognostics.
3. The Planets. Chap. II.
4. Popular Fallacies in Questions of Physical Science.

Part II., price 5d.
5. Latitudes and Longitudes.
6. The Planets. Chapter III.
7. Lunar Influences.
8. Meteoric Stones and Shooting Stars. Chap. I.

Part III., price 6d.
9. Railway Accidents. Chap. I.
10. The Planets. Chap. IV.
11. Meteoric Stones and Shooting Stars. Chap. II.
12. Railway Accidents. Chap. II.
13. Light.

VOLUME II., *price 1s. 6d., in handsome boards.*

Part IV., price 5d.
14. Common Things. Air.
15. Locomotion in United States. Chap. I.
16. Cometary Influences. Chap. I.
17. Locomotion in the United States. Chap. II.

Part V., price 5d.
18. Common Things. Water.
19. The Potter's Art. Chap. I.
20. Locomotion in the United States. Chap. III
21. The Potter's Art. Chap. II.

Part VI., price 6d.
22. Common Things. Fire.
23. The Potter's Art. Chap. III.
24. Cometary Influences. Chap. II.
25. The Potter's Art. Chap. IV.
26. The Potter's Art. Chap. V.

☞ *The Work is continued in Weekly Numbers at 1d., in Monthly Parts at 5d., and Quarterly Volumes at 1s. 6d, in Ornamental Boards.*

LONDON: WALTON & MABERLY,
UPPER GOWER STREET, AND IVY LANE, PATERNOSTER ROW.

PEACE AND WAR, by SIR E. LANDSEER,
THE COMPLETION OF THE VERNON GALLERY.

THE ART-JOURNAL:
MONTHLY JOURNAL OF THE FINE ARTS: THE ARTS OF INDUSTRY, &c. &c.

Volumes One to Five of the NEW SERIES, comprising the Vernon Gallery, are now ready, and may be obtained, together or separately, at the price of One Guinea and a Half, bound in cloth, &c.; each Volume contains Thirty-six Engravings on Steel, and upwards of Six Hundred Engravings on Wood.

The SIXTH VOLUME, to be issued during the year 1854, will complete the entire series of the •VERNON GALLERY—the great national collection of the works of British artists—the munificent gift of Mr. Vernon to the British people. Among those yet to appear are several of the most valuable and interesting of the Gallery; for example:—

Peace and War, by Landseer.
Hamlet, by Maclise.
The Saviour Prophesying over Jerusalem, by Eastlake.
The Dame School, by Webster.

The Grape Gatherers in the South of France, by Uwins.
The Hall at Courtray, by Haghe.
Lord William Russell, by Johnston.
&c. &c.

With the Volume for 1854 will be also given, in association with those choice examples of the VERNON GALLERY, Line Engravings of the following works by leading masters of the British and foreign schools:—

Raising the Maypole, and A Summer's Holiday, after F. Goodall, A.R.A.
View in Italy, after C. Stanfield, A.R.A.
Job and his Friends, after P. F. Poole, A.R.A.

Val St. Nicola, after J. D. Harding.
The Death of Nelson, after Slingeneyer.
Van de Velde studying after Nature.
&c. &c.

VIRTUE, HALL & VIRTUE, 25, PATERNOSTER ROW.

RELIGIOUS TRACT SOCIETY,
56, PATERNOSTER ROW, AND 164, PICCADILLY.

WEEKLY PERIODICALS.

The Sunday at Home. A Family Magazine of Instruction and Recreation. 16 pages super-royal 8vo, with superior Engravings. Price One Penny; or in Monthly Parts, Fivepence.

The Leisure Hour. A Family Journal of Instruction and Recreation. super-royal 8vo, with superior Engravings. Price One Penny; Monthly Parts, Fivepence.

EDUCATIONAL WORKS.
12mo, cloth, boards.

The History of England, to A.D. 1852. By T. MILNER, M.A., F.R.G.S. Two Maps.

The History of Greece, to A.D. 1833. By the Rev. PROFESSOR STOWELL, D.D. With a Map. 2s. 6d.

The Bible Handbook; an Intro- duction to the Study of Sacred Scripture. By JOSEPH ANGUS, D.D. With a Map. 5s.

The History of Rome to the Fall of the Empire. By T. MILNER, M.A., F.R.G.S. Maps. 12mo, 3s., cloth, boards.

Lives of Illustrious Greeks. By the Rev. PROFESSOR STOWELL, D.D. 3s.

A Universal Geography : in Four Parts—Historical, Mathematical, Physical, and Political. By T. MILNER. M.A., F.R.G.S. Ten Coloured Maps, with Diagrams, by A. PETERMANN, F.R.G.S.

Athens: its Grandeur and Decay. Fcap. 8vo. Engravings. 2s. cloth, boards, 2s. 6d. gilt edges.

Eastern Arts and Antiquities. 16mo, 3s. 6d. cloth boards.

Remarkable People; the Arab, Jew, and Egyptian. 16mo. Engravings, 4s. cloth, boards.

Rome (City of); its Edifices and its People. Engravings. Fcap. 8vo, 2s. 6d. cloth, boards, 3s., extra.

Stoughton's Palace of Glass. Royal 18mo, 2s. cloth, boards.

CHEAP POCKET VOLUMES.
18mo, with Frontispiece, each 1s. 6d., cloth, boards.

ANCIENT EGYPT AND TYRE—BABYLON AND NINEVEH—COURT AND PEOPLE OF PERSIA, By Dr. KITTOE—LONDON IN ANCIENT AND MODERN TIMES—AUSTRALIA; ITS SCENERY, RESOURCES, &c. &c.

₊ The Catalogues of the Society may be obtained on application at the Depositories.

SOLD BY THE BOOKSELLERS.

GLASS SHADES

FOR THE PROTECTION OF ALL ARTICLES WHICH MAY BE INJURED BY EXPOSURE,
WHOLESALE AND RETAIL, AT
CLAUDET AND HOUGHTON'S,
89, HIGH HOLBORN, LONDON.
Lists of Prices (which have been greatly reduced) will be forwarded free, on application.

PLATE GLASS, PATENT PLATE GLASS,
SHEET AND CROWN WINDOW GLASS,
Hartley's Rough Plate Glass and Horticultural Sheet Glass
FOR CONSERVATORIES, ETC.,
PAINTED AND STAINED GLASS.
And every variety of Coloured and Ornamental Window Glass.

CLAUDET AND HOUGHTON,
89, HIGH HOLBORN, LONDON.
Lists of Prices or Estimates sent free on application.

CABINET, UPHOLSTERY, EASY CHAIR, AND CARPET MANUFACTORY,
28 & 32, BERNERS STREET, MIDDLESEX HOSPITAL,
CRYSTAL PALACE, FURNITURE COURT, NUMBERED 27, 28, AND 29.

T. H. FILMER respectfully announces that his large range of Ware-rooms are replete with the most modern and elegant FURNITURE, including a great variety of Cabinets, Writing Tables, Escritoires, and Flower Stands, in Buhl, Marqueterie, &c., manufactured of thoroughly seasoned materials and superior workmanship. In the Upholstery and Carpet Department will be found every description and quality of material from designs of the most eminent artists, and executed by the first manufacturers, both native and foreign. Upwards of 200 Easy Chairs, Sofas, and Couches always in stock, warranted stuffed with the best materials.

The entire Stock for price, quality, variety, and extent is not surpassed by any house in the kingdom.

ESTABLISHED 1820.
28 & 32, BERNERS STREET, MIDDLESEX HOSPITAL.

GLENFIELD PATENT STARCH,
USED IN HER MAJESTY'S LAUNDRY,
WOTHERSPOON'S SCOTCH MARMALADE,
Jams, Jellies, Lozenges, and Comfits, made by Machinery.
(Which gained the Prize Medal of 1851.)

May be had of all Grocers, wholesale of WOTHERSPOON, MACKAY, & Co., 66, Queen-street Cheapside, London.

DR. COLLYER'S

CALIFORNIA QUARTZ CRUSHER,

TRITURATOR, AND GOLD EXTRACTOR.

Patented in the United States, Great Britain, France, and other European Countries.

SCALE ONE-EIGHTH OF AN INCH TO THE FOOT.

MANUFACTURED BY

RANSOMES AND SIMS, IPSWICH.

EXPLANATION.

THE power or driving wheel of a 10-horse engine is attached to the arm of the large cylindrical roller, situated in the curved basin. When motion is given, a slow, undulating, vibratory, partial rolling and sliding action, is communicated to the cylinders; these operate as *crushers*, *triturators*, and *pulverizers*, by their weight and rubbing, as well as crushing motion. The large cylinder is six feet in diameter, and its weight is between six and seven tons. The smaller cylinder is three-and-a-half feet in diameter, and its weight between three and four tons. The weight of either cylinder may be increased one-third by being filled with sand or water. They are so constructed that when one portion becomes worn by long use, a new surface may at once be presented by changing the fulcrum. All parts of the machine are of great strength and durability. The figure of a man feeding the machine with ore is seen in the above cut, and at the same place a constant stream of water is represented as flowing into the basin. After the ore has been reduced by the large cylinder, it passes with the water through a coarse screen to the smaller cylinder, or triturator, where it is thoroughly rubbed and scoured, and again passes a fine screen of 2500 meshes to the square inch. The crushed ore next enters the Amalgamator Proper, where, by the repeated revolution of corrugated cylinders, it is so thoroughly incorporated with the mercury (heated by steam) that, on analysis of the *tailings*, no trace of gold can be discovered.

The machine works over 350 square feet of crushing and triturating surface per minute, being equivalent to the crushing action of 30 heads of stamps, each weighing 500 lb.

The trituration of the gold particles is absolutely necessary, otherwise the mercury cannot become associated with them. The amalgamating process has been tested in California for three years with the most perfect success. Each machine will reduce 20 tons of hard ore per diem.

A full sized machine is now being erected at Messrs. JOHN TAYLOR AND SON'S Establishment, Rotherhithe, where Mining Companies, or those desirous of having auriferous ores tested, can have experiments made on a large scale, so as to arrive at a commercial estimate of the value of their Mines.

For further particulars address, DR. COLLYER, the Patentee, at the Mining Journal Office, 26, Fleet Street, or

MESSRS. RANSOMES AND SIMS, IPSWICH.

ART-UNION OF LONDON,

444, WEST STRAND.

INSTITUTED 1837.

INCORPORATED BY ROYAL CHARTER, 10th VICTORIÆ 1846.

PRESIDENT.

THE RIGHT HONOURABLE THE LORD MONTEAGLE.

PLAN FOR THE CURRENT YEAR.

Every Subscriber of One Guinea for 1854-5 will be entitled to :—

I. AN IMPRESSION OF A PLATE by J. T. WILLMORE, A.E.R.A., from the original picture by J. J. CHALON, R.A.,—

"A WATER PARTY."

II. A VOLUME OF THIRTY WOOD ENGRAVINGS, by leading Artists, illustrating Subjects from LORD BYRON'S—

"CHILDE HAROLD."

III. THE CHANCE OF OBTAINING ONE OF THE PRIZES to be allotted at the General Meeting in April next, which will include—

> THE RIGHT TO SELECT FOR HIMSELF A VALUABLE WORK OF ART FROM ONE OF THE PUBLIC EXHIBITIONS;
>
> STATUETTES IN BRONZE OF "HER MAJESTY ON HORSE-BACK," by T. THORNEYCROFT;
>
> COPIES IN BRONZE, from a Model in relief, by R. JEFFERSON, of "THE ENTRY OF THE DUKE OF WELLINGTON INTO MADRID;"
>
> STATUETTES IN PORCELAIN OR PARIAN;
>
> PROOF IMPRESSIONS OF A LARGE LITHOGRAPH, by T. H MAGUIRE, after the original picture, by W. P. FRITH, R.A., "THE THREE BOWS," from Molière's "BOURGEOIS GENTILHOMME."

Post-office orders sent in payment of Subscriptions must be made payable at the Post-office, Charing Cross, to THOMAS SIMONS WATSON, the Assistant Secretary.

June 1, 1854.

GEORGE GODWIN, } *Honorary*
LEWIS POCOCK, } *Secretaries*

d

The Council or First Class Medal for superior excellence in General Brass Founding, Metallic Bedsteads, and Gas Fittings, &c., was awarded by the Jurors of Class 22, in the Great Exhibition of 1851, to:

R. W. WINFIELD,

CAMBRIDGE STREET WORKS, METAL ROLLING AND WIRE MILLS
BIRMINGHAM.

PROPRIETOR OF THE ORIGINAL PATENT FOR

METALLIC MILITARY BEDSTEADS,

PATENTEE AND MANUFACTURER OF OTHERS UPON IMPROVED PRINCIPLES
PATENTEE OF THE

NEW PROCESS FOR THE ORNAMENTATION OF METALS;
AND MANUFACTURER OF

BRASS DESK, PEW, ORGAN, AND OTHER RAILING;
WINDOW CORNICES, PATENT CURTAIN BANDS AND ENDS;
GLASS CORNICE RINGS; LOCOMOTIVE RAILINGS AND MOULDINGS;

BRASS AND ZINC NAME-PLATES FOR SHOP FRONTS;
SASH BARS AND WINDOW GUARDS;

CANDLE CHANDELIERS AND SCONCES;

PATENT TUBES, BY THE NEW PATENT PROCESS, WHETHER TAPER OR DOUBLE;

Picture, Pulley, Curtain, Wardrobe, & Stair Rods, Astragals, & Beading;
WINDOW FRONTS, MOULDINGS, PLATES, AND GUARDS;

BALUSTRADES;
FIRE SCREEN STANDS AND ARMS;
BONNET, HAT, CLOAK, AND UMBRELLA STANDS;

BRASS AND IRON RECLINING AND OTHER CHAIRS;
GAS CHANDELIERS, PILLARS, BRANCHES, AND FITTINGS
of all kinds, and in various styles;
TUBING OF EVERY DESCRIPTION, ROUGH AND FINISHED;

BRASS AND COPPER WIRE, AND ROLLED METALS.

SHOW ROOMS.
CAMBRIDGE STREET WORKS, BIRMINGHAM; AND
141, FLEET STREET, LONDON.

R. W. WINFIELD'S NEW AND EXTENSIVE SHOW ROOMS contain Specimens of his Patent Metallic Military Travelling, and House Bedsteads, so much in use at home and abroad, with many other Articles of Furniture in Brass, Bronze, Or-Molu, and imitation of Silver; together with Gas Fittings of every description, and a variety of other articles of his Manufacture.

The Portable Bedsteads are admirably adapted for use in the Camp, or for Travelling; also well suited for Officers in the Army and Navy.

THE PATENT SHIP COT AND SOFA is recommended to Invalids and Officers refitting; it will be found to prevent Sea-Sickness, and afford all the comfort of a Bed upon Shore.

d 2

THE CRYSTAL PALACE,
SYDENHAM.

MR. G. BAXTER, the Inventor and Patentee of Oil Colour Picture Printing, begs to announce that he has in preparation a Series of Views of the Exterior and Interior of the Crystal Palace; including faithful representations of the Egyptian, Pompeian, and other Courts. They will be printed in Oil Colours, and each Picture will be published and sold, by special desire of the Directors, by GEORGE BAXTER, at the Palace, Sydenham.

THE ELECTRIC TELEGRAPH COMPANY.
INCORPORATED 1846.
THE CRYSTAL PALACE
has been placed in direct communication with

The Electric Telegraph Company's System in Great Britain
and with that on the Continent, by means of

THE INTERNATIONAL TELEGRAPH COMPANY,
so that Messages can be transmitted between the Crystal Palace and any Telegraph Station in Great Britain, Ireland, or the Continent of Europe.

The Electric Telegraph Company's Office is on the left hand side of the Grand Entrance with access from the outside.

By order,
Lothbury, London, June, 1854.   J. S. FOURDRINIER, Secretary.

COMFORT TO THE FEET. EASE IN WALKING

THE LEATHER CLOTH.
Or, PANNUS CORIUM BOOTS AND SHOES,

are the easiest and most comfortable ever invented for Tender feet; a most valuable relief for Corns, Bunions, Gout, Chilblains, &c., having no drawing or painful effect on the wearer, and adapted for all climates

A Boot or Shoe sent for size will ensure a Fit. The material sold by the yard in any quantity.

SUPERIOR VULCANISED INDIA RUBBER OVERSHOES, with soles which prevent sliding.

HALL & CO., Patentees, Wellington Street, Strand, London, leading to Waterloo Bridge; and No. 5, South-west Gallery, Crystal Palace.

CAUTION.—TO TRADESMEN, MERCHANTS, SHIPPERS, OUTFITTERS, &c.—WHEREAS it has lately come to my knowledge, that some unprincipled person or persons have for some time past been imposing upon the public, by selling to the Trade and others a spurious article under the name of

BOND'S PERMANENT MARKING INK.

This is to give notice, that I am the Original and sole Proprietor and Manufacturer of the said article, and do not employ any Traveller, or authorise any person to represent themselves as coming from my Establishment for the purpose of selling the said Ink.

This Caution is published by me to prevent further imposition upon the public, and serious injury to myself.

E. R. BOND,
SOLE EXECUTRIX AND WIDOW OF THE LATE JOHN BOND,
28, LONG LANE, WEST SMITHFIELD, LONDON.

BRADLEY'S PALE OR BITTER ALE.
Genuine and in Fine Condition, as recommended for invalids and the table by the Faculty.

BRADLEY & Co. beg to inform the Trade, that they are now registering Orders for March Brewings of their Pale Ales, in casks of 18 gallons and upwards, at the Soho Brewery, Sheffield, and at their undermentioned Establishments,—141, High-street, Hull; 43, South John-street, Liverpool; 2, Palace-street, Manchester; White Horse-yard, Chesterfield; Marsh Gate, Doncaster.

ROYAL PANOPTICON
OF
SCIENCE AND ART,
LEICESTER SQUARE.

OPEN DAILY FROM 12 TO 5.

EVENINGS (SATURDAYS EXCEPTED) FROM 7 TO 10.

ADMISSION, ONE SHILLING.

GREAT ORGAN, LECTURES,
MACHINERY IN ACTION, ELECTRICITY, &c., &c., &c

PHOTOGRAPHIC DEPARTMENT OPEN DAILY.

THE following OLD-ESTABLISHED and HIGHLY-ESTEEMED PREPARATIONS can be recommended as suitable and valuable in all climates :—

BUTLER'S TASTELESS SEIDLITZ POWDERS,

Combined in one Compound Powder, in bottle and case (accompanied with measure and spoon) at 2s. 6d., suitable for all climates, efficacious and most agreeable.

BUTLER'S CONCENTRATED SARSAPARILLA,

Containing all the properties of the Sarsaparilla in a very condensed state, in pints, half, and quarter pint bottles. A pint bottle is equal to three gallons of the ordinary preparation.

BUTLER'S VEGETABLE TOOTH POWDER,

Pre-eminent for preserving and beautifying the teeth, properties which have procured for it the approbation of the most distinguished personages in the United Kingdom. Sold in boxes at 2s. 9d.

BUTLER'S TARAXACUM, OR DANDELION COFFEE.

An agreeable and efficacious mode of using the Taraxacum in Affections of the Liver, Kidneys, and Digestive Organs. In Tins at 2s. 6d.

BUTLER'S MEDICINE CHEST DIRECTORY.

Family, Sea, and Government Medicine Chests fitted up with appropriate Medicines and Directions, for all climates.

BUTLER & HARDING, Chemists, 4, Cheapside, corner of St. Paul's, London.

CUTLERY AND SHEFFIELD PLATE,

WARRANTED OF FIRST-RATE QUALITY.

JOSEPH MAPPIN & BROTHERS,

QUEEN'S CUTLERY WORKS, SHEFFIELD.

STOCK IN LONDON AT 37, MOORGATE STREET;

GOODS ON SHOW

IN THE

SHEFFIELD COURT of the CRYSTAL PALACE.

Buyers of CUTLERY, ELECTRO-PLATED GOODS, AND DRESSING CASES, are invited to the London Warehouse, 37, MOORGATE-STREET, where an immense variety of Stock can be seen of MESSRS. MAPPINS' own manufacture.

MESSRS. MAPPIN are appointed Cutlers to Queen Victoria, and were honoured with a Prize Medal at the Great Exhibition of all Nations in 1851, for the superior quality and excellence of their manufactures.

JOSEPH MAPPIN & BROTHERS,

QUEEN'S CUTLERY WORKS, SHEFFIELD;

AND

37, MOORGATE STREET, LONDON.

PARASOLS.

THE demand for a much better and more elegant description of PARASOLS having prevailed during the last few years,

W. & J. SANGSTER

have again had manufactured in Lyons and Spitalfields, to their order, some rich and costly patterns, of which they respectfully invite an inspection. W. & J. S. also beg to say they have received from Canton another parcel of China Crape Parasol Covers, made expressly for this house, which article was so much admired last season.

Alpaca Parasols are particularly recommended for the sea-side and garden, on account of their great durability.

140, Regent Street.	10, Royal Exchange.
94, Fleet Street.	75, Cheapside.

EXTREMELY LIGHT UMBRELLAS FOR LADIES, ON FOX'S PARAGON FRAMES.

PHILOSOPHICAL DEPARTMENT,
No. 69 A.

RICHARD READ,

Instrument Maker, by special appointment, to Her Majesty,

35, REGENT CIRCUS, PICCADILLY, LONDON.

The Offices for the Collecting and Legally Recovering Rents.
ESTABLISHED UPWARDS OF 60 YEARS.

MR. HARDING, Auctioneer and Appraiser, 25, New Broad Street, London, having the honour of transacting business for the Corporation, several Worshipful Companies, and many of the most influential citizens in London, begs respectfully to call the attention of Landlords and others to the above Offices, where their interests will be carefully studied.

BY APPOINTMENT TO THE QUEEN AND ROYAL FAMILY.

PATENT PERAMBULATORS.

C. BURTON, INVENTOR, PATENTEE, AND SOLE MANUFACTURER.

THE distinguished patronage, the flattering encomiums, and the increasing demand, are sufficient proofs of the utility and excellence of these fashionable, safe, and elegant Carriages for adults, children, and invalids, propelled from behind by the slightest effort.

Illustrated Circulars.
Shipping Orders.
Office, 487, New Oxford-st.

THE BEST BLACK TEA (Congou), 3s. 8d. per lb.; Good ditto, 2s. 8d., 3s., 3s. 4d.; Souchong, 4s.; The Finest Lapsang, 4s. 4d.; Orange Pekoe, 4s. 4d.; Young Hyson or Gunpowder from 3s. Ceylon, Plantation, and Costa Rica Coffees, 1s., 1s. 4d., and 1s. 6d. per lb.; the Finest Old Mocha, 1s. 8d.

Carriage paid by Rail to any part of England on Teas and Coffees to the amount of 40s., and on general orders to the amount of £5. List of Prices sent free on application.

MARSHALL & SON, GROCERS TO THE QUEEN,
GLOBE TEA WAREHOUSE, 20, STRAND.

THE ARGYLL GENERAL MOURNING WAREHOUSES,

246 & 248, REGENT STREET.

THE Proprietors of the ARGYLL GENERAL MOURNING WARE-
HOUSES respectfully beg to intimate to Ladies, whose bereavements demand the immediate
adoption of Mourning Attire, that every requisite for a complete outfit of Mourning can be supplied
by them at a moment's notice, and that many unpleasant occurrences arising from delay on melancholy occasions are by these means obviated. That all trouble may be also avoided in deciding upon
the degree of Mourning proper to be worn under various losses, the Proprietors have published a
book, entitled "Mourning Etiquette," giving in detail every requisite rule and direction, and which
may be had gratis by addressing to them.

TIME OF NOTICE IN ORDERING MOURNING.

If all Dresses, made complete, 12 hours.
If Bodices of Dresses, unmade, a moment's notice is sufficient.

D. NICHOLSON & COMPANY.

SOUTH EASTERN RAILWAY,

The Direct Mail Route to all Parts of the Continent, with the Shortest Sea Passage.

DAILY COMMUNICATION BETWEEN LONDON AND PARIS IN TWELVE HOURS;

London and Brussels in Fourteen Hours;
London and Cologne in Twenty Hours;
Sea Passage only Two Hours.

SUMMER SERVICES, 1854.

LONDON TO PARIS BY TIDAL TRAINS
VIA FOLKESTONE AND BOULOGNE.

This is the quickest and most comfortable means of communication between London and Paris; it is performed every day, the time of departure varying in accordance with the tide. (Time Table published daily in front page of "The Times.") The Passengers are conveyed by Express Train to Folkestone, where they find a powerful Steamer waiting in the harbour to receive them; they walk on board, and two hours afterwards are landed at Boulogne, where another Train is in readiness to convey them immediately to Paris. The whole journey is thus accomplished without interruption, in the shortest possible time, no small boats for embarking and disembarking being required.

By these Trains, luggage can be registered for Paris direct, relieving the Passenger from all trouble about it until the arrival in Paris, and avoiding the Customs examination at Boulogne.

The same correspondence of Trains and Steamers is arranged for the journey from Paris to London.

Fixed Continental Services via Dover and Calais.

FROM LONDON.

LONDON	depart	8.10 a.m.	*11.30 a.m.	*8.30 p.m.
Dover	„	11. 0 „	2.30 p.m.	11.15 „
Calais	„	2 30 p.m.	6 30 „	3. 0 a.m.
PARIS	arrive	9.40 „	5. 5 a.m.	10. 0 „
BRUSSELS	„	10.10 „	5. 0 „	10.50 „
COLOGNE	„	5. 0 a.m.	1.30 p.m.	4.45 p.m.

TO LONDON.

COLOGNE	depart	11.30 p.m.	6.15 a.m.	*9.30 a.m.
BRUSSELS	„	7. 0 a.m.	2. 0 p.m.	3. 0 p.m.
PARIS	„	7. 0 „	11.45 „	7.30 „
Calais	„	3. 0 p.m.	10. 0 „	2.30 a.m.
Dover	„	7.30 „	2. 0 a.m.	5.20 „
LONDON	arrive	10.15 „	4.50 „	7.45 „

* These Trains are not direct on Sundays.

Offices for Through Tickets, Time Bills, &c. :—

In LONDON—40, Regent Circus, Piccadilly;
In PARIS—4, Boulevard des Italiens;
In BRUSSELS—74, Montagne de la Cour.

G. S. HERBERT, *Secretary.*

London Bridge Terminus, May, 1854.

EAGLE
INSURANCE COMPANY.
3, CRESCENT, NEW BRIDGE STREET, BLACKFRIARS, LONDON

DIRECTORS.

ROBERT ALEXANDER GRAY, Esq., *Chairman.*   THOMAS DEVAS, Esq., *Deputy-Chairman.*

CHARLES BISCHOFF, Esq.   JOSHUA LOCKWOOD, Esq.
THOMAS BODDINGTON, Esq.   W. ANDERSON PEACOCK, Esq.
NATHANIEL GOULD, Esq.   RALPH CHAS. PRICE, Esq.
CHAS. THOS. HOLCOMBE, Esq.   THOS. G. SAMBROOKE, Esq.
RICHD. HARMAN LLOYD, Esq.   WILLIAM WYBROW, Esq.

Auditors—THOMAS ALLEN, Esq.   JAMES GASCOIGNE LYNDE, Esq.

Physician—GEORGE LEITH ROUPELL, M.D., F.R.S., 15, Welbeck-street.

Surgeons—JAMES SANER, Esq., M.D., Finsbury square.   WM. COOKE. Esq., M.D., 39, Trinity-square, Tower-hill.

Bankers—Messrs. GLYN, MILLS & CO., 67, Lombard-street.   Messrs. HANBURYS & LLOYDS, 60, Lombard-street.

Actuary and Secretary—CHARLES JELLICOE, Esq.

The Business of the Company comprises Assurances on Lives and Survivorships, the Purchase of Life Interests, the Sale and Purchase of Contingent and Deferred Annuities, Loans of Money on Mortgage, &c.

THIS Company was established in 1807, is empowered by the Act of Parliament 53 Geo. 3, and regulated by Deed enrolled in the High Court of Chancery.

The Company was originally a strictly Proprietary one. The Assured, on the participating Scale, now participate quinquennially in four fifths of the amount to be divided.

To the present time (1853) the Assured have received from the Company, in satisfaction of their claims, upwards of £1,400,000.

The amount at present assured is £3,000,000 nearly, and the income of the Company is about £125,000.

At the last Division of Surplus, about £120,000 was added to the sums assured under Policies for the whole term of Life.

The lives assured are permitted, in time of peace, and not being engaged in mining or gold digging, to reside in any country,—or to pass by sea (not being sea-faring persons by profession) between any two parts of the same hemisphere—distant more than 33 degrees from the Equator, without extra charge.

All Policy Stamps and Medical Fees are now paid by the Company.

By recent enactments, persons are exempt, under certain restrictions, from Income Tax, as respects so much of their income as they may devote to assurance on Lives.

The Annual Reports of the Company's state and progress, Prospectuses and Forms, may be had, or will be sent, post free on application at the Office, or to any of the Company's Agents.

SOVEREIGN
LIFE ASSURANCE COMPANY,

49, ST. JAMES'S STREET, LONDON.

ESTABLISHED 1845.

This Office presents the following advantages :—

The security of a large paid-up Capital.

Very moderate rates for all ages, especially young lives.

No charges whatever, except the premium.

All Policies indisputable.

Advances made to Assurers on liberal terms.

By the recent bonus, four-fifths of the premium paid was in many instances returned to the policy holders. Thus :—On a policy for £1,000, effected in 1846, premiums amounting to £153 8s. 4d. had been paid, while £123 7s. was the bonus added in 1853.

A weekly saving of 14d. will secure to a person 25 years of age the sum of £100 on his attaining the age of 55, or at death, should it occur previously.

Rates are calculated for all ages, climates, and circumstances connected with life assurance.

Prospectuses, forms, and every information can be obtained at the—

Office, 49, St. James's Street, London.

HENRY D. DAVENPORT, *Secretary*.

SOUTH AUSTRALIAN BANKING COMPANY.

INCORPORATED BY ROYAL CHARTER, 1847.

54, OLD BROAD STREET, LONDON.

The Directors grant Letters of Credit and Bills on *Adelaide*, payable in cash.
Bills on South Australia collected and negotiated.

AGENTS.

HALIFAX.—Commercial Banking Company.
HULL.—Hull Banking Company.
LIVERPOOL.—Borough Bank, and Messrs. TRIMMER & GRAINGER.
PLYMOUTH.—J. B. WILCOCKS, Esq.
SOUTHAMPTON.—Hants Banking Company.

WILLIAM PURDY, Manager.

ALLIANCE

BRITISH AND FOREIGN

Life and Fire Assurance Company,

BARTHOLOMEW LANE, LONDON.

Capital £5,000,000 Sterling.

ESTABLISHED 1824.

Board of Direction.

PRESIDENTS.

SAMUEL GURNEY, Esq. | SIR MOSES MONTEFIORE, Bart.

DIRECTORS.

G. H. BARNETT, Esq.	SAMUEL GURNEY, JUN., Esq.
SIR E. N. BUXTON, Bart.	JOHN IRVING, Esq.
SIR ROBERT CAMPBELL, Bart.	SAMPSON LUCAS, Esq.
SIR GEORGE CARROLL.	THOMAS MASTERMAN, Esq.
RIGHT HON. G. R. DAWSON.	SIR A. N. DE ROTHSCHILD, Bart.
JAMES FLETCHER, Esq.	L. N. DE ROTHSCHILD, Esq., M.P.
CHARLES GIBBES, Esq.	OSWALD SMITH, Esq.
WILLIAM GLADSTONE, Esq.	MELVIL WILSON, Esq.

AUDITORS.

ANDREW JOHNSTON, Esq.—JOSEPH M. MONTEFIORE, Esq.—GEORGE PEABODY, Esq.

Life Assurances are granted under an extensive variety of forms, and with or without participation in profits.

The Lives of Military and Naval Men, not in actual service, are assured without extra charge ; and no additional premium is payable for service in the Militia.

Stamps on Life Policies are paid for by the Company.

Loans are granted on the sole security of the Company's Policies, when of sufficient value to justify an advance of £50 or more.

Fire Assurances are accepted at the usual rates ; and Foreign Assurances, both Life and Fire, on reasonable terms.

Detailed Prospectuses will be furnished on application.

F. A. ENGELBACH, Actuary & Secretary.

HAND-IN-HAND FIRE AND LIFE INSURANCE SOCIETY,

No. 1, NEW BRIDGE STREET, BLACKFRIARS, LONDON.

INSTITUTED IN 1696.—EXTENDED TO LIFE INSURANCE 1836.

IMMEDIATE, DEFERRED, AND SURVIVORSHIP ANNUITIES GRANTED.

Directors.

The Hon. WILLIAM ASHLEY.	JAMES ESDAILE, Esq.	WILLIAM SCOTT, Esq.
The Hon. SIR EDWARD CUST.	HARVIE M. FARQUHAR, Esq.	JOHN SPERLING, Esq.
ARTHUR EDEN, Esq.	JOHN GURNEY HOARE, Esq.	HENRY WILSON, Esq.
JOHN LETTSOM ELLIOT, Esq.	E. FULLER MAITLAND, Esq.	W. ESDAILE WINTER, Esq

Auditors.

The Hon. COLONEL CUST. | JAMES ESDAILE, Esq. | THOMAS FULLER MAITLAND, Esq

Bankers.
Messrs. GOSLINGS AND SHARP, 19, Fleet Street.

Physician.
THOMAS K. CHAMBERS, M.D., 1, Hill Street, Berkeley Square.

Standing Counsel.
The Honourable A. J. ASHLEY, 32, Lincoln's Inn Fields.

Solicitors.
Messrs. NICHOLL, SMYTH, & Co., 18, Carey Street.

Actuary.
JAMES M. TERRY, Esq.

Secretary.
RICHARD RAY, Esq.

LIFE DEPARTMENT.

The important advantages offered by the plan and constitution of the Life Department of the Society are :—

That Insurers are protected by a large invested Capital, upon which there is no Interest to pay, and for which no deduction of any kind is made; which enables the Directors to give the whole of the Profits to insuring Members.

That the Profits are divided annually amongst all Members of five years' standing, and applied towards reducing Life Insurance to the lowest possible rates of Premium.

The following Table exhibits the abatement of Premium that has been made for the past Twelve Years to Members of Five Years' standing :—

Years of Division.	Rate of Abatement.	Years of Division.	Rate of Abatement.
1842	£45 per Cent.	1849	£52½ per Cent.
1843	45 ,,	1850	52½ ,,
1844	45 ,,	1851	52½ ,,
1845	50 ,,	1852	52½ ,,
1846	50 ,,	1853	52½ ,,
1847	50 ,,	1854	52½ ,,
1848	50 ,,		

That persons insuring their own lives, or the lives of others, may become Members.

That persons who are willing to forego participation in the Profits can insure at a lower rate than that charged to Members.

No charge for Policy Stamps.

FIRE DEPARTMENT.

Insurances are effected on every description of property at the usual rates.

(By order)   RICHARD RAY, *Secretary.*

INDISPUTABLE LIFE POLICY COMPANY,

72, LOMBARD STREET, LONDON.

TRUSTEES.

RICHD. MALINS, Esq., Q.C.,M.P. | JOHN CAMPBELL RENTON, Esq.
JAMES FULLER MADOX, Esq. | RICHARD SPOONER, Esq., M.P.
                    WILLIAM WILBERFORCE, Esq.

THE Policies of this Company being indisputable (in terms of the Deed of Constitution duly registered) are TRANSFERABLE SECURITIES, their validity not being dependent upon the import of past, and perhaps forgotten, circumstances, and office documents. Used as FAMILY PROVISIONS, they relieve the assured from all doubt and anxiety as to the future.

	Sums Assured.	New Premiums.		Sums Assured.	New Premiums.
1849	£108,617	£4,364	1852	115,195	4,296
1850	110,215	3,974	1853	123,093	4,532
1851	127,488	4,438		ALEXANDER ROBERTSON, Manager.	

NATIONAL PROVIDENT INSTITUTION,
48, GRACECHURCH STREET, LONDON,
FOR MUTUAL ASSURANCE ON LIVES, ANNUITIES, &c.

DIRECTORS.
CHAIRMAN—Samuel Hayhurst Lucas, Esq.
DEPUTY CHAIRMAN—Charles Lushington, Esq.

John Bradbury, Esq.	John Feltham, Esq.	Robert Sheppard, Esq.
Thomas Castle, Esq.	Charles Gilpin, Esq.	William Tyler, Esq.
William Miller Christy, Esq.	Robert M. Holborn, Esq.	Charles Whetham, Esq.
Edward Crowley, Esq.	Robert Ingham, Esq., M.P.	

PHYSICIANS.
J. T. Conquest, M.D., F.L.S. | Thomas Hodgkin, M.D.

TRUSTEES.
John Feltham, Esq. | Samuel H. Lucas, Esq.
Robert Ingham, Esq., M.P. | Charles Lushington, Esq.

ARBITRATORS.

Henry Compton, Esq.	John Geo. Malcolm, Esq.	John Tidd Pratt, Esq.
Josh. C. Dimsdale, Esq.	Richard Ogle, Esq.	James Vaughan, Esq.
John James, Jun., Esq.	Thomas Paley, Esq.	

BANKERS—Messrs. Brown, Janson, and Co., and Bank of England.
SOLICITOR—Septimus Davidson, Esq.
CONSULTING ACTUARY—Charles Ansell, Esq., F.R.S.

Extracts from the REPORT of the Directors for 1853 :—

"The Directors congratulate their fellow-members on the very gratifying result of the recently-completed Quinquennial Investigation of the assets and liabilities of the Institution, by which it appears that, on the 20th November, 1852, after providing for the present value of all the liabilities in the Life Assurance Department, a surplus remained of £242,627, which has been duly apportioned as heretofore.

"The reductions range from 5 to 89 per cent. on the original Annual Premiums, according to the age of the party and the time the policy has been in force; and the Bonuses vary in like manner, from 59 to 75 per cent. on the amount of Premiums paid during the last five years.

"The total amount of the reductions per annum for the ensuing five years is £33,348 17s. 2d.

"The Bonuses assigned to those policies on which the original Premiums continue to be paid amount to £89,880 5s.; this, together with Bonuses apportioned at former divisions, makes an aggregate addition to the sums assured by the Policies in force of £126,564.

"Notwithstanding the great reduction of Premiums, the net annual income arising from 12,326 existing Policies is £163,912 7s. 1d.; this sum, with the interest on invested capital, viz., £37,298 7s. 3d., shows a total annual income of £201,210 14s. 4d."

The amount of CAPITAL exceeds ONE MILLION STERLING.
Prospectuses and all other information may be obtained on application to the Office.
March 18, 1854.   JOSEPH MARSH, Secretary.

EVERETT'S BLACKING,
51,
FETTER LANE, LONDON.

Used at the Palace, and in the Establishment of every man of *ton* in the kingdom.

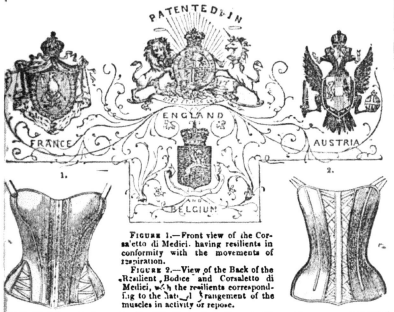

WS - #0023 - 280322 - C0 - 229/152/13 [15] - CB - 9780265548714 - Gloss Lamination